40

RAF LYNEHAM

Hercules Super Station in Action

RAF LYNEHAM

Hercules Super Station in Action

Wilf Pereira

Foulis

Haynes

A **FOULIS** Aviation Book

First Published 1990

Published by:
Haynes Publishing Group
Sparkford, Nr Yeovil, Somerset
BA22 7JJ

Haynes Publications Inc.
861 Lawrence Drive, Newbury Park,
California 91320, USA

British Library Cataloguing in Publication Data
Pereira, Wilf
RAF Lyneham: Hercules Super Station in Action
1. Great Britain. Royal Air Force. Aerodrome. Royal Air Force
Lyneham
I. Title
358.4170942
ISBN 0-85429-767-7

Library of Congress catalog card number 90-83294

Design: Mike king
Editor: Mansur Darlington
Printed in England by: J.H. Haynes & Co. Ltd
Typeset in 11 on 11 point Rockwell light roman
condensed

Contents

ACKNOWLEDGEMENTS

Acknowledgements should go first to those RAF Lyneham personnel who provided every assistance with this book. Naming all the helpers would create too long a list yet they have to be thanked collectively for their generous contributions

Some names however must be mentioned. These include Wing Commanders Tony Ford and Clive Cooper who, as successive officers in charge of Lyneham's Administration Wing, made the overall arrangements. Then there were Squadron Leader Ernie Dunsford and Flight Lieutenant Ted Querzani who, as successive Community Relations Officers, put the arrangements into effect. Thanks must also be expressed to Corporal Bob Stonehouse of the Station's Photographic Section, the many Wings and Squadrons, plus everyone else providing the illustrations. The photographs in Chapter 1 and 12 are the authour's except where otherwise noted all other illustrations are Crown copyright reserved.

Last but not least, my special thanks to Squadron Leader Chris Bartle formerly of the Hercules Training Squadron and now of 70 Squadron. Whilst the book was in preparation he had the responsible task of training pilots on Lyneham's flight simulators and aircraft. Looking after me as well must have been an added chore. Despite his duty-packed days, Chris treated me with promptness, efficiency and invariable good humour. In fact he proved the truism that if one wants a job well done give it to a busy man.

RAF LYNEHAM VITAL STATISTICS

Covers 2,500 acres
3.5 miles of runways
690 work buildings
1,000 married quarters
61 Lockheed C-130 Hercules
24-hour-a-day, 365-day-a-year operation
3,500 Service and civilian personnel
14,000 sorties flown a year
150,000 passengers carried a year
18,000 tons of freight carried a year
12,000,000 gallons of aviation fuel used a year

LOCKHEED C-130 HERCULES CMk3 VITAL STATISTICS

Length 112 ft 9 in (34.37 m)
Wing span 132 ft 7 in (40.57 m)
Tailplane span 52 ft 8 in (16.05 m)
Height 38 ft 3 in (11.66 m)
Propeller diameter 13 ft 6 in (4.11 m)
Engines 4 Allison T56-A-15 4,508 ehp (3,362 kW)
turboprops
Max cruising speed 374 mph (602 km/h)
Max normal take-off weight 155,000 lb (70,310 kg)
Range with maximum payload 2,356 miles (3,791 km)
Capacity:
38,900 lb (17,645 kg) of freight or
7 cargo pallets or
4 vehicle and 4 trailers or
128 troops or
92 paratroops or
97 stretcher cases

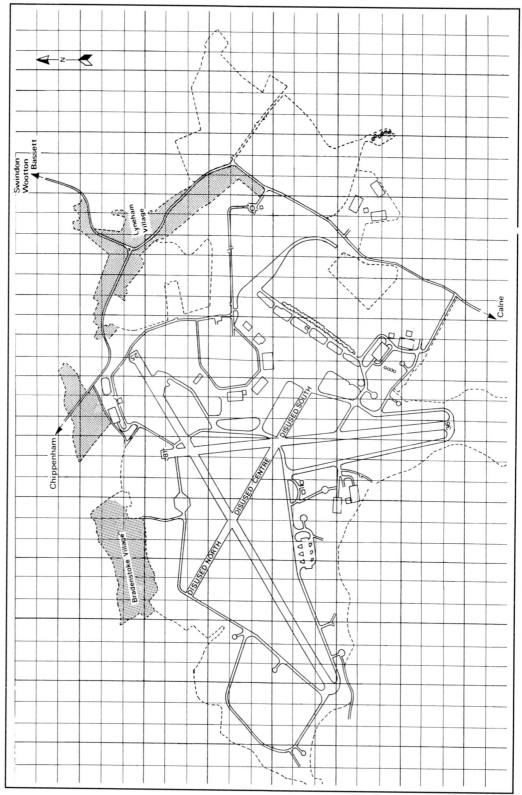

This map of RAF Lyneham shows the general layout of the station, runways and perimeter tracks.

8

Chapter 1
SQUADRON MOVE

Sunday morning 0330 hours. The Wiltshire villages around RAF Lyneham are fast asleep, but the station never rests. Lights line its roads, shine from hangars and key buildings. Floodlights mounted on pylons illuminate a concreted expanse, known as the pan, where rows of Hercules transport aircraft are parked. The scene is deceptively tranquil until armed sentries step out of shadows to check passes. On the airfield beyond the pan security police patrol with guard dogs. At the far side of the base, Lyneham air traffic controllers keep constant watch from their tower overlooking the runways and from below in the radar room.

The operational centre of Lyneham is the Air Terminal next to the pan. This is a low level building with only a ground and first floor. On the ground floor passengers are assembled then taken to the waiting aircraft. First floor facilities include the station's Operations Room, Meteorological Office and Flight Planning. The last contains maps and information for aircrews setting out on their allocated journeys. At 0330 hours on this Sunday morning there are four people in the room. One is a member of the flight planning staff wearing RAF working uniform. The other three are in flying gear bearing their ranks, names and trades.

Flight Lieutenant Adrian Keen, a No.47 Squadron Pilot, is to be Captain of forthcoming Flight 4478. Accompanying him are Flying Officer Paul Morris, Co-Pilot and Flight Lieutenant Derek Johnson, Navigator, both also of No.47 Squadron. Without wasting a word, their Flight Captain outlines the task ahead. They are to assist an exercise called a Squadron Move. To them, it is a routine and relatively simple operation. The simple term 'Squadron Move' describes what is, in fact, a complex operation.

Royal Air Force commitments include the swift and efficient shifting of whole squadrons. With planes it is easy. They simply fly from A to B. Modern-day aircraft, however require considerable technical support. Therefore staff, stores and specialised equipment must quickly follow. This particular squadron move, Adrian Keen states, is to take freight and personnel from Kinloss, Scotland to an airfield 'Somewhere in Norway'. A second Lyneham Hercules will be leaving in an hour's time on the same task. It will be manned by instructors from the station's No.242 Operational Conversion Unit which trains crews to fly Hercules. Thus 242 OCU instructors will be helping out with the operation as well as honing their own flying skills.

As it is early on a Sunday morning, Adrian Keen continues, and civil air traffic is minimal, the first leg of the flight will be direct to Kinloss. The route will run diagonally across a broad air traffic band, known as an airway, normally crowded with civil aircraft, which extends up the backbone of Britain. His designated aircraft – Hercules 292 – has sufficient fuel to reach Kinloss. There it will take on fuel for the second and third legs of the journey. Maps are unfolded. The pilots and navigator confer, make calculations and confer again.

Above: Flt Lt Adrian Keen of No.47 Squadron and Captain on Flight 4478 confers with Flt Lt Derek Johnson his Navigator for the Squadron Move.

Above right: Flying Officer Paul Morris, Co-Pilot, carrying out his calculations and inputs to the operation.

It all looks unhurried, but the hands of a wall clock are moving relentlessly towards 0500: take-off time.

The initial stage of flight planning over, the three go along the corridor to the Meteorological Office. Inside, a bank of screens show weather patterns and progressions in full colour. Nearby print units are producing up-to-the-minute data. The Met man on duty describes what Flight 4478 can expect. First he refers to peripheral conditions. There are thunderstorms moving up from Biscay towards Cornwall and Ireland. However, high pressure remains steady over Britain and Scandinavia. The flight should enjoy near perfect weather. One peculiarity is stressed, a rare occurrence. Ground temperature is 10°C, but at 1000 feet this rises to 20°C. The move into warmer, less dense air can cause loss of engine power so the condition must be anticipated and rectifying action taken. The two pilots nod. Finally the Met man hands over a comprehensive illustrated print-out of weather affecting the route.

Back in Flight Planning, Adrian Keen systematically takes his two colleagues through the contents of a thick blue-covered loose-leaf folder. It is the Task Diary that has been compiled to contain every item bearing on the flight. The Captain has previously studied the diary, yet he goes over it once more. The task is defined. There are route details, crew information, transport arrangements, inter-service signals and diplomatic clearances. Every agency touched by the trip will have been notified, every agreement to co-operate confirmed. In this way the station authorities at Kinloss, the squadron being moved, the units moving them and the Norwegians receiving them are all alerted. As Captain, Co-Pilot and Navigator leave Flight Planning, they pass a similar trio from No.242 OCU entering to commence work on the second stage of the same overall exercise.

Downstairs two activities allied to the first flight have taken place. Seven men from yet another Lyneham unit stand ready and waiting. They are members of the United Kingdom Mobile Air Movements Squadron (UK MAMS). Their duties comprise dealing with passengers and particularly freight, also to go anywhere at any time. The team standing by is made up of auxiliaries – that is, part-time servicemen. An equally well planned task lies ahead of them. They will load the first aircraft at Kinloss, three members will accompany it to Norway for unloading while four remain at the Scottish base to load the second aircraft. Then, after that, too, has been unloaded in Norway, the second plane will return to Lyneham with the magnificent seven. The other activity at the entrance to the Air Terminal is the presence of motor transport to take all concerned out to Hercules 292. This aircraft is a CMK1 version which is 15 feet shorter than the CMK3 which has two extra fuselage sections fore and aft of the mainplane. Hercules 304 nearby, to be flown by the second crew on the same exercise, is a CMK3.

At Hercules 292, three more crew members emerge to confer with their Flight Captain.

They are Master Air Loadmaster Hugh Thomas, Sergeant Air Engineer Chris Kennedy and Flight Lieutenant Tony Mortimer, also an Air Engineer. All are from No.47 Squadron. Aboard the aircraft, Hugh Thomas is responsible for everything from Bulkhead 245 back to the aircraft's rear ramp/door assembly. In other words he looks after the Hercules hold, its loading, security and unloading. Here he will be helped by the seven men from UK MAMS. Chris Kennedy is to be the Flight Engineer sitting directly behind and between the Captain and Co-Pilot. As for Tony Mortimer – Chris's chief – he is there to lend a supporting hand. It is a fine attitude, one found throughout Lyneham. As Tony himself expressed it: 'Chris is young, trained and gaining experience by the minute. There is no doubt he can do his job. I am merely here to help and to pass on the flight engineering experience I acquired in the same way.'

For the past two hours, Chris and Tony have been working their way through their pre-flight checks, as has Loadmaster Hugh Thomas. With the arrival of pilots and navigator, the six men quietly become a single team. Adrian Keen and Paul Morris occupy the left- and right-hand pilots' seats respectively, while Derek Johnson moves to his navigator's station in the starboard rear corner of the flight deck. All don headsets by which they can communicate during engine run-up, take-off and flight.

Take-off is on schedule at 0500 hours. The empty Hercules soon leaves the runway and noses through the morning mist. It pierces the layer of warm air at 1000 feet and continues to climb unconcerned at a rate of 2000 feet a minute. A cloud layer is similarly pierced to bathe aircraft and crew in the dazzling dawn. The light is already so strong that green sun visors are clipped over the starboard windows. Presently Hercules 292 levels out at 26,000 feet. Cloud formation over the Midlands is thinning and the countryside below resembles the maps beside pilots and navigator. Adrian identifies towns and roads. The M6 motorway runs northwards like a ruled route marking. In an amazingly short time, he is pointing out the Lake District with Haweswater a blue mirror lying on grey-green fells.

Breakfast is served to all aboard. It starts and ends with piping hot coffee. In between comes chilled orange juice, grapefruit segments with a cherry for each helping, sausages and bacon, warm croissants, real butter, chunky marmalade. Hugh Thomas keeps producing food from an aluminium box as if he is a master conjurer. The crew eat in rotation, remaining at their stations. Technical conversation over the head sets is interspersed by complimentary remarks about Lyneham catering.

Exactly on 0630 hours, Hercules 292 touches down at Kinloss. Paul Morris makes the approach and landing under the eye of the more experienced Adrian Keen. Similarly Chris Kennedy in the flight engineer's seat has his chief Tony Mortimer beside him. Both supportive roles are of an encouraging rather than inhibitive nature. Adrian has amassed eight years experience on Hercules, first as a co-pilot with No. 30 Squadron, then as a captain at No.47. Tony joined the RAF at the age of 17 and his service career covers the engineering spectrum from fitter to instructor.

The airfield at Kinloss is bathed in sunshine. Along its northern perimeter lies the Moray Firth, the water sparkling, the strand shining round Burghead Bay. The airfield itself is quiet, as befits the morning of a Scottish Sabbath, though deceptively so. Most of the Kinloss-based maritime reconnaissance aircraft are parked and only duty personnel can be seen. Only one corner shows signs of activity as several large trailers, piled high with stores, are being towed to an open area.

No sooner is Hercules 292 parked nearby and the engines cut than Hugh Thomas lowers the rear ramp. A cable from a power winch, located at the forward end of the hold, is taken out to the first and heaviest trailer. Once that is aboard, the others are physically loaded by the men from UK MAMS. Briskly, box after heavy box is lifted, carried into the hold and stacked. Boxes cover the width of the floor apart from a narrow passageway on each side. The pile of boxes grows towards the hold ceiling. Trailer and boxes are netted, the latter in sections, to prevent shifting during flight. Nets are hauled tight by tensioners secured

Hercules 292 arrives at Kinloss by the Moray Firth to take on squadron freight and personnel, also fuel.

Freight and fuel for the Squadron Move converge on the aircraft precisely to the task timetable.

to the hold floor. Other items are cunningly stored in the hold: spare landing gear tyres, filing cabinets, tools and tool kits. Eventually there is little room left vacant but the narrow side-walks and the ramp itself. These are now to be filled.

A coach arrives containing 30 personnel from the squadron on the move with their personal baggage. Their number includes aircrews, engineering technicians and a WRAF – the squadron's adjutant. Their bags are piled, netted and secured on the ramp, after which squadron members file fifteen a side along the hold where there are let-down canvas benches. The space is so limited, they can only stretch their legs by standing. Once inside, it is difficult to pass one another, but all are joking. Hugh, who never seems to stop working throughout the long day, raises the rear ramp.

While all this is taking place, the rest of Hercules 292 crew are performing a series of tasks. The pilots make visual checks inside and outside the aircraft. The navigator is laying out maps and reference books for the next stage of the journey. The two engineers are equally busy. One has produced a ladder from somewhere (the Hercules seems to be a fully-equipped self-contained workshop as well as a heavy duty pantechnicon and a versatile flying machine) and is inspecting the turboprop engine tailpipes. The other has turned his attention to the refuelling operation because a large tanker with an equally large trailer is approaching the starboard side of the aircraft exactly on schedule.

It is interesting how the two engineers, without any apparent consultation, assist each other wherever needed. For example, when one opens a small inspection panel on the inner port engine, the other hands up a flashlight. In the same way, when one fits the refuelling hose to the aircraft inlet connection (near the aft end of the starboard main landing gear fairing) the other automatically goes on the flight deck to double check the gauges. The fuelling operation takes some 10-15 minutes, NATO F34 aviation fuel – a close relation to paraffin – being delivered at 185 gallons a minute.

Personnel of United Kingdom Mobile Air Movements Squadron (UK MAMS) commence loading.

Moving a squadron involves such items as spare wheels and a long inventory of other components.

Personal kit of servicemen on the move loaded and safety netted on the Hercules loading ramp.

During this period, the second Lyneham Hercules 304 touches down at Kinloss. Like everything else, it is on schedule. The aircraft is taxied to a nearby position where more squadron equipment personnel and another refueller with trailer awaits it. One begins to acquire the idea that Kinloss is more active than appears on an early Sunday morning. Nothing is hurried yet everything gets done quickly. If there is any small hold-up or difficulty, everyone lends a hand.

During the short stopover at Kinloss, between their very different though interconnected work patterns, people talk of the reasons for squadron moves, also of those they have known. In the case of maritime reconnaissance work, this is practised from the two extreme ends of the United Kingdom – namely, from Cornwall and Scotland. NATO commitments require flight operations from Norwegian bases to cover important sea sectors. Thus strategic requirements have to be converted to tactical practicalities. Even on a fine summer's day, a squadron move entails upheavals and hard efforts. Judging from the tales told, it is incomparably harder during the depths of winter when aircraft and crews are contending with high winds and heavy snows.

Young Paul Morris, the flight's co-pilot, quietly listens to and takes in these conversations. He is still on his learning curve. He says: 'Three years ago I was working in a garden centre. I often thought of flying for the RAF and one day decided to give it a try. It entailed 18 weeks of Initial Officer Training at Cranwell followed by 14 months Flying Training. This I began again at Cranwell, then at

On the left is Flt Lt Tony Mortimer from No. 47 Squadron who helped Chris on this flight.

Tony Mortimer and Chris Kennedy manhandling the hose from the fuel bowser to the Hercules inlet connection.

Arrival of Lyneham Hercules 304 at Kinloss for the second stage of the Squadron Move.

Finningley. The trainer aircraft were Jet Provosts and the turboprop-powered Jetstream. Lyneham was my first real posting. Like every other pilot arriving to fly Hercules, I spent six months at the Operational Conversion Unit. Eventually, in December 1988, I joined No.47 Squadron.' There followed flights taking him all over Europe and across the Atlantic – a long way from that garden centre.

Tony Mortimer speaks more of flight engineers than himself (he joined, long before Paul, straight from a Yorkshire farm): 'The standard of flight engineers is high, yet it keeps improving. The new intakes have good 'O' and 'A' Levels. They are sharp and gain confidence rapidly. Take young Chris for example. He has already acquired the ability to put over his engineering expertise to experienced pilots, to call the shots when difficult technical decisions have to be made. It is a pleasure rather than a duty to help such youngsters succeed.' Tony nods, his eye on Chris who is systematically inspecting the aircraft main landing gear. 'That lad's married, lives near Lyneham and his wife is also in the Air Force – a Loadmaster on VC10's. Some people moan about kids nowadays, but give them the opportunities and they can amaze us.'

It is now 0815 hours. Hercules 292 has been loaded, inspected and fuelled. The passengers are aboard and the crew back on the flight deck. All has been accomplished without a single order. The pilots settle in their seats, the engineers continue with their technical rituals, the navigator hands out new maps. Down aft, moving around the crowded hold, the loadmaster ensures that everything is secure, everyone reasonably comfortable.

After he has done so – at the precise psychological moment – Hugh Thomas decides that passengers and crew can do with drinks. Non-alcoholic of course. He commences another of his conjuring acts. Tea or coffee, orange squash or coke. Hot plastic cupfuls and well chilled cans keep materialising and are passed along lines with snippets of service humour, 'Sorry, no gin.' – 'You'll get fat wanting sugar.' – 'Slimline Coke then.' – Hugh produces a Slimline Coke as if it is one of his easier tricks.

On the flight deck radio contacts are being made, fuel usage established, route details finalised. The impression, though it seems like a contradiction in terms, is that of casual professionalism. On analysis, this is due to thorough training and practice. Despite the banter, small points tell. Route maps are carefully folded and clipped in position. The flight engineer wears gloves, fire retardant ones, because powerful electrics are concealed behind instrument panels. All are aware of potential dangers – high pressure hydraulics, high revving turbines working at high temperatures. That is why six eyes – those of the two pilots and the flight engineer – constantly check the banks of dials. Synchronisation is safety. Deviation is incipient danger, to be detected and rectifying action taken.

Outside the aircraft, a Kinloss ground crew has arrived to assist in engine starting supervised by Hugh Thomas. As each turbine is spun, the Hercules – like a dozing dog awaiting its master – quivers eagerly awake. The crew on the flight deck goes unhurriedly through sequences learned in lecture rooms, on simulators and training flights. Revs, temperatures and pressures are noted, adjusted, fine tuned. At 0840 hours, when Hercules 292 begins to roll, it does so past 304 in the middle of the second loading operation. More trailers with crates, personnel with travel bags, are participating in the squadron move. They smile and wave as 292 goes past them. Adrian Keen with his left hand on the nose gear steering wheel and his right on the throttles guides the aircraft to the black-and-white striped patch at the beginning of the runway.

At 0845 hours, the Hercules carrying a full load of freight and passengers, lifts easily away from Kinloss and heads north eastwards across the Moray Firth. The coast falling away behind the aircraft changes colour from bright green to dark grey. Similarly the blue expanse of sea alters to resemble pewter that has been fine hammered then highly polished. The Hercules is indifferent to these delicacies of colours and shadings. It is eager to show off its rate of climb, now at a steady 1500 feet a minute. Its blunt nose thrusts through successive layers of sea mist and cloud strata. Eventually 292 levels out at 21,500 feet showing no signs of exertion. Cabin pressure and temperature remain perfectly comfortable. At 0900 hours, Hugh Thomas is about to perform another of his conjuring tricks with food. He moves among crew and passengers asking, 'Would you like ham or chicken sandwiches?' They are handed round and much appreciated.

About this time, the WRAF adjutant from the squadron on the move comes to the flight deck. She likes to see the flight deck of each RAF plane on which she travels.

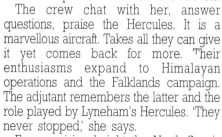

The crew chat with her, answer questions, praise the Hercules. It is a marvellous aircraft. Takes all they can give it yet comes back for more. Their enthusiasms expand to Himalayan operations and the Falklands campaign. The adjutant remembers the latter and the role played by Lyneham's Hercules. 'They never stopped,' she says.

From cruising height the North Sea is empty and lonely apart from the solitary speck of a ship leaving the faintest of white wakes. Curved patterns, extending over many miles, are pervading the silvered surface. These swirls represent immense currents thrust between the Caithness mainland and the Orkney Islands by the fetch of the Atlantic. The Captain indicates a misty green shape looking like a leaf adrift on the sea, then points to his map. 'Fair Isle.'

After Fair Isle drifts away, there is little to see from the flight deck and certainly nothing from the well-packed hold with its few windows. There the squadron-move

Squadron personnel in the Hercules' hold – with beer supplies prominent in the foreground.

passengers doze, read, munch sandwiches and sip fruit juices. They half sit, half lie, their feet wedged against the central load. Occasionally someone gets up and stretches. Officers and other ranks share the same conditions. Master Air Loadmaster Hugh Thomas passes among them miraculously not disturbing anyone. Someone asks him if he knows how much the Hercules is carrying. Of course he knows. 'Twenty thousand pounds of freight and fourteen hundred of baggage.'

These and other facts, including information on passengers and crews, are included in the paperwork Hugh manages to complete. He does so quickly and concisely amid what appears to be impossible conditions. The tops of crates, spare areas of floor not occupied by feet, even bits of fuselage wall not taken up by pipes and cable runs, are his various desks. His office is as mobile as the squadron.

From 0945 hours onwards, a strange sight begins to manifest itself on the eastern horizon. Previously, where silver sea met colourless sky, there was no clear cut line, just an indeterminate band indicating the horizon. Now strange white specks appear along the band as if some celestial artist is dabbing them on it.

Gradually the specks grow in number and size. They coalesce, form groups, fill the band. From the panoramic view afforded by the many large windows of the Hercules flight deck, the white patterns are discerned to be dazzling snowpeaks above dark troughs running steeply down to bleak serpentine waters. These are the mountains and fjords of Norway from which the dreaded Vikings of long ago sailed in their longships to Britain, Ireland, Greenland and America.

At this stage, detailed maps of the coast are produced, also the Hercules crew are happy to be in the capable hands of Norwegian air traffic control. Both kinds of assistance are necessary for the shore line is more intricately serrated and labyrinthine than can be imagined. Snow fields surmount sheer cliffs that dive deep into the Norwegian Sea. Promontories like gnarled fingers, convoluted islands of all shapes and sizes, a weird mix of jagged and glacier ground rock beds slide past under the aircraft. Whenever possible – and sometimes among the seemingly impossible – roads wind their way round steep slopes, skirt abrupt precipices, bridge dark waters to link islands, tiny hamlets and remote houses. Such

The view from the flight deck of Hercules 292 as it approaches the islands and fjords of Norway.

The vista over snow-capped mountains on route to a designated airfield 'somewhere in Norway'.

feats represent centuries of effort of which the Norwegians can be justly proud.

Following this spectacular coast northwards, Captain Adrian Keen confers with Co-Pilot Paul Morris over the intercom system. The former has made the trip many times. It is the young co-pilot's first overview. Landmarks are identified: higher mountains, deeper fjords and larger islands. The air base destination is not easy to locate let alone to land at. It lies behind a snow-laced mass with the runway angled from the approach direction. A detailed landing chart from Lyneham's flight planning room is produced. It gives runway alignments, lengths, control tower location, taxiways and parking sites. The Captain clips it in front of him.

A steep bank and descent are followed by a featherlight touchdown. It is as if the Hercules is not a heavily laden four-engined transport but a single-engine flying club aircraft. Next comes a long period of taxying where taxiway widths become narrower and narrower. Towards the end of this, two crew members crouch by the side windows to check the wing tips passing close to huts and pylons. Despite such complications, Adrian Keen taxies the Hercules with its 132 foot wing span as if motoring in a Mini. At last he reaches the required parking place, brakes gently and cuts the engines.

Moments later the tailend ramp is lowered and the offloading of squadron personnel, baggage, stores and equipment commences. To start with the ramp is fully lowered so that people can walk down it. The tensioned net covering the bags is released and these are collected by their owners. Then the ramp is raised to a horizontal position and a hefty metal stool placed under the rear edge. The ramp is now hydraulically locked and mechanically supported at truck bed level. Norwegian Air Force motorised platforms – a cross between a fork lifter and a low loader – come rolling out of a nearby hangar. A small adjustment for height and they are in business. Once more the squadron artefacts are moved by hand. Clearing the Hercules hold looks a formidable task, which it is, but UK MAMS and willing helpers soon manage to reduce the stacks. Eventually the stool is removed, the ramp lowered again and the trailer that went in first is offloaded last. The minutiae of off-loading is managed by Hugh Thomas from start to finish.

No sooner has he cleared the hold than he begins collecting, counting and storing all the articles recently utilised. Nets are folded, straps secured, a multiplicity of fittings placed in special boxes and lockers. While he is engaged on this, the second Lyneham Hercules 304 comes whispering onto the runway and rolls along the various taxiways to join aircraft 292. Its ramp is lowered, more squadron personnel file out followed by their luggage. They begin the unloading of their freight. By now Hugh has completed his good housekeeping process. He closes the rear doors, checks the security of all locks then, without a pause, begins asking the crew, 'Steak or chicken for your Sunday dinner?'

Hercules 304 had arrived around 1200 hours and shut down its engines. By 1215 hours the engines of 292 are running. Chocks are withdrawn, brought into the aircraft and the door shut. By 12.30 hours Hercules 292 is airborne and climbing at 2000 feet a minute. An air of satisfaction as well as an aroma of Sunday dinner pervades the flight deck. The steaks from the galley cooker prove tender, the croquette potatoes in a tomato and mushroom sauce positively mouthwatering. The first course is followed by apple pie and cream, cheese and biscuits, excellent coffee. Someone congratulates Hugh Thomas on the dinner.

Paul Morris in the co-pilot's seat, talking to his Captain during the return flight to Lyneham.

'Not me,' he says. 'It's Lyneham in-flight catering going from strength to strength.'

'Could show the civil airlines a thing or two,' someone else agrees and a third adds, 'Club class.'

Afterwards, Master Air Loadmaster Thomas is relatively still at last, completing his paperwork. After that, he talks of his RAF career. Following eight years on helicopters (Pumas, Chinooks and Wessex) he applied for a Lyneham posting because his home is at nearby Melksham. It was worth a try, he said, and he got it. Now following 18 months on Hercules, he is due to start a two month Tactical Support course. When? Tomorrow. Where had he been during his year and a half at Lyneham? Just about everywhere. Where especially? 'Well, there was the Hercules support for the Tornado round-the-world exercise. We got as far as Hong Kong then were diverted back to Nepal on earthquake relief work. This Norway trip is routine, as are those to Germany, the Middle East and the United States. I was also on one of the last Hercules air bridges to the Falklands.' About the changeover from the Wessex to the Hercules he said: 'In the Air Force they are affectionately known as Walter and Albert. Both strong, dependable, made to work. You throw what you want into them, then off you go. Great! I'm glad to have known Walter and Albert.'

As he talks, the captain has taken Hercules 292 up to 31,000 feet to show the young co-pilot how it handles at that altitude. This also saves fuel. The Hercules (or Albert) does not seem to care. It flies just as well higher than Everest. Cabin pressurisation and temperature are just as comfortable despite the thin sub-zero conditions outside. The North Sea far below

looks like a perfectly planed sheet of metal. Presently the surface seems to acquire stains. These are in reality approaching shallows – sandbanks and weedbeds. The ever eager aircraft is already at the English coast by the Humber Estuary.

The letdown for Lyneham begins over Lincolnshire, a farmer's patchwork quilt with a predominance of yellow oil-seed rape. Flight Lieutenant Adrian Keen points out RAF Cranwell where so many crew members commenced their flying careers. Not long afterward he is indicating the Oxford to Birmingham road. Albert is eating up the miles. The aircraft is already within Lyneham's 40 mile radar net.

At 1515 hours the landing gear is lowered. From the flight deck, Hercules 292 appears to be on a shallow slide which will deposit it on the Lyneham runway. Touchdown is barely audible. Reverse thrust is louder but not noticeably fierce despite tons of aircraft coming to a halt within seconds. Then it is rolling again, on to the pan, towards its allotted slot among long lines of other Alberts.

As the crew of Hercules 292 disembark, 304 arrives nodding on the pan. Despite their hour handicap at the beginning of the operation, the instructor crew of No.242 OCU show they know a thing or two about making up time.

Ground crews immediately take over both aircraft. Transport is standing by to ferry crews to the Air Terminal. Then Lyneham springs a last surprise. De-briefing is left until the morrow. Already the crews are fanning out across

Master Air Loadmaster Hugh Thomas with his headset and 'umbilical cord' during engine shutdown.

the car park. Tony Mortimer murmurs something about catching the end of a village cricket match. Adrian Keen mentions seeing family friends who had come over for tea. He makes the concentrated efforts of the last twelve hours – flying the length of Britain, crossing the North Sea, finding his way through the maze of Norway's mountains and islands then heading straight back to Lyneham – seem simple. Which it is to trained teams working together. The day's task was a squadron that needed moving. So they moved it.

Chapter 2
RURAL LOCATION

Visitors to RAF Lyneham mostly come by car; or by train then car. A great many fly in, but more of that later. The usual land journey is westward out of London either along the M4 motorway or by InterCity en route from Paddington to Bristol. Both these means of transport take similar paths. To begin with the London suburbs stretch on as if forever past Heathrow, between Slough and Windsor. Only from Reading onwards is the countryside discernible. Here the motorway cuts great swathes through the Berkshire Downs while the railway curves northwards to follow the Vale of the White Horse. Road and rail near each other again at Swindon. Train travellers for Lyneham transfer to motor transport and again head westwards to meet the M4 at Junction 16.

From Junction 16, visitors head towards Wootton Bassett. At the large roundabout leading into this busy little community, the road signs are joined by another more authoritative one pointing to RAF Lyneham. Wootton Bassett itself has a wide main street with a noticeable half-timbered building supported by stone columns near the far end. This is the Town Hall which was originally constructed in 1700 and restored in 1889. The first Sir Winston Churchill, father to the Duke of Malborough had a nearby residence.

Wootton Bassett and its distinctive town hall built in 1700 lies three miles from Lyneham.

The road out of Wootton Bassett descends a long hill and from there it is three more miles to RAF Lyneham. Even in that short final lap, visitors often experience the feeling of entering another more ancient country. For Wiltshire, in which the modern air base is currently sited, has a heritage that goes back into the mists of time. It contains fascinating towns and villages, the country's most beautiful cathedral at nearby Salisbury, and the three mightiest Stone Age monuments in Europe: Avebury, Silbury and Stonehenge.

Although RAF Lyneham is well signposted, one can easily drive past it and continue across the beckoning Wiltshire landscape. The driver simply sees the entrance before the road curves. As for travellers on the nearby motorway and railway, the air base is completely invisible. This is because they are down in the Vale of Dauntsey, through which the Wiltshire Avon meanders, while Lyneham occupies a plateau hidden behind the wooded brows of several hills. Yet Lyneham itself is the fifth largest town and the fourth highest rate payer in the county. Its presence is only betrayed by aircraft constantly rising from and sinking back on to the still invisible airfield. However, before entering the main gate, one should take a quick look at some of the villages surrounding Lyneham. This is because all are associated with one of the largest and most active stations operated by the Royal Air Force.

Lyneham is situated in the centre of a rough square with corners at Wootton Bassett, Malmesbury, Chippenham and Calne. A brief history of Lyneham Village is given in the next chapter as an introduction to the station's history. So here the perimeter communities will be covered to give the reader a feel for the place. Malmesbury to the north-east claims to be the oldest borough in England, inhabited for more than a thousand years. Now its ruined abbey and picturesque market place stand high above the Avon. Chippenham is another market town with history going back to Saxon times and the claim that King Alfred the Great once lived there. Calne was known as a stopping place for stage coaches travelling between London and the West Country.

More immediate to Lyneham are the villages ringing it. RAF personnel live in all these villages and contribute much to the welfare of their respective communities. Moving clockwise from the Somerfords in the north, the ring of villages and hamlets include the Tockenhams, Hilmarton, Christian Malford and Bradenstoke. The last lies next to the north-west perimeter of the airfield. Here are a few interesting facts about these typical Wiltshire dwelling places.

Little and Great Somerford are about half a mile apart with the Wiltshire Avon winding between them. In the summers of long ago the stream could be forded during dry periods – hence the name. Since then the main London-Bristol railway line passes by the south end of Little Somerford then over the river. Despite their closeness to each other the two Somerfords are dissimilar in appearance. Little Somerford is built round crossroads with its church at the railway line end of the village. Great Somerford is made up of two parallel roads amid a network of paths and paddocks. In fact this whole area of North Wiltshire stretching to the South Cotswolds is noted for its fine farms, manor houses and horse-loving inhabitants.

Like the two Somerfords there are two Tockenhams. The road from Wootton Bassett to Lyneham passes between Tockenham Wick to the north and plain Tockenham to the south. A 16th century map shows the latter as West Tockenham possessing a Tockenham Court and a Tockenham House. Nowadays there is a Tockenham Court Farm and a Queen Court Farm occupying the old sites. Since then manor rights and church benefices have linked and unlinked the Tockenhams with Lyneham. The latest links include the many air base families who have their homes in these nearby communities.

Hilmarton, some three miles south of Lyneham, is a particularly attractive village with its church on one side of the lane and a manor farmhouse on the other. The church tower has four slender corner pinnacles and inside there is a fine ceiling. A war memorial window links the figures of St. George and General Gordon. Again, many local inhabitants either work at or have connections with RAF Lyneham and the same applies to Christian Malford.

The latter has grown steadily, what with new houses for working and retired couples. One interesting development is laid out in small groups of closes to further community relations. Christian Malford church is perched on a bluff above the Avon. It has an elegant tower and a medieval screen across the chancel.

Other interesting habitations with their churches and cottages, inns and shops, manor houses and fine farms lie all around RAF Lyneham. Intriguing names abound: Foxham, Goatacre, New Zealand, Swallett Gate and Idover Demesne, Sodom. But nearest to the airfield, after Lyneham itself, is Bradenstoke. This village, looking over the motorway and Avon Valley to the Cotswold Hills is very attractive. It has several timber-framed buildings with projecting upper stories and thatched roofs, a church and two inns.

Bradenstoke has been well researched by enthusiastic historians serving at RAF Lyneham. Much was discovered in and around the old abbey. At one time its lands included the then villages of Malmesbury and Chippenham. Two fascinating details are all we have room for here. During investigations of the abbey ruins, a seven-foot skeleton was found walled-up near the main entrance. The remains are believed to be those of a monk who loved a local lady and paid the price. This monk is also believed to have haunted the area for centuries. The second story is more down to earth. Prior to the air base, there was a footpath over the fields between Bradenstoke and Lyneham. Beside the path stood stones where coffins could be rested during conveyance from one village to the other. If those bearers could have looked into the future they would have seen an unbelievable world of large aircraft, broad runways and strange buildings round them. Nowadays the station covers over 2500 acres on which stand some 690 buildings plus 1000 married quarters.

Which brings us to the centre of these rural locations and the subject of this book. Three-quarters of the population in present-day Lyneham Village are RAF personnel and their families. The married quarters, with roads bearing famous aviation names as Trenchard and Tedder, form part of the community. There are shops and a NAAFI, a school for over

Lyneham parish church, which serves both village and air base, and has a resident RAF chaplain.

500 children, the churches of England, Scotland and Rome. St. Michael's, the parish church, has an RAF Chaplain who serves also at Bradenstoke. This church and churchyard adjoins the station and many of its services are official occasions conducted with due ceremony. Visitors will immediately note the many Air Force connections including the altar table decorated with squadron badges. Outside, across the churchyard the gravestones of servicemen stand in stark white rows.

At one time the main entrance into RAF Lyneham was from the Bradenstoke lane at the other side of the airfield. As the base expanded during World War II and concrete runways laid over what had once been meadowland, the Bradenstoke gate was closed and the present one from Lyneham Village substituted. This left an old guardroom stranded in the middle of the base. From the windows of No.242 Operation Training Unit's convivial crewroom, one can see the original front-pillared guardroom. There, in the 'bad old days', gimlet-eyed Service Policemen would inspect airmen before allowing them to leave the station and inflict themselves on the civilian world. Woe betide anyone with dirty buttons, overlong hair or what was called an 'unairmanlike appearance'. To make the point, a full length mirror was affixed to the outside wall of the guardroom so that airmen could make last-minute adjustments before stepping inside for their leave passes.

The present day main guardroom at RAF Lyneham is much more practical. It has to be in order to process hundreds of service and civilian personnel, cars and coaches in and out of the base. It is especially business-like about security. Armed guards patrol the environs of the main gate – as they do everywhere round the airfield – automatic rifles at the ready. Checks are always thorough. The interiors of cars, car boots and the undersides of vehicles are likely to receive the full treatment. Guardroom staff, firmly but politely, insist on confirmations of identity and require known personnel to accompany visitors at all times. Telephone checks take place in back rooms. The process is continuous and unremitting because RAF Lyneham is always on duty.

Once past the guardroom, the first sight greeting the visitor is that of a Comet four-jet aircraft standing on a nearby lawn – and thereby hangs a Lyneham tale. Following the Comet 1 disasters when a number of these aircraft literally fell out of the sky, the aviation world was aghast. How the fatigue problem was identified and solved is well known today. What should be equally well-known was how the RAF acquired, flew and proved Comet 2s all over the world. The Royal Air Force still flies other versions of the Comet, in the form of the Nimrod Airborne Early Warning System while Lyneham, having played its part, went on to help develop air transportation with its Hercules. The Comet on the lawn is a reminder of an operation satisfactorily completed. One day perhaps a Hercules will stand in its place.

To the left of the Comet is the Officer's Mess, a spacious and relaxing place. The unremitting work outside is not obvious within its walls. Instead one senses an atmosphere of service and continuity notably lacking in too many other areas of our modern-day world. There are elegant lounges and bars, a fine dining room, also a special area for the WRAF officers who have important roles in the running of the station.

To the right of the main entrance is the station's Medical Centre. This provides the high standard of health facilities for which the Royal Air Force has always been noted. The centre at Lyneham looks after all personnel and their dependants. These include everyone on the station and in its married quarters. When personnel and their families arrive, they register at the centre to which medical records have been sent. When they leave Lyneham, the centre automatically sends the documents to their new medical officer or doctor. Arrangements are available for emergencies, home visits, ante-natal and child care. Examinations for full fitness take place at least annually while innoculations and vaccinations are daily occurrences. The latter are necessary due to personnel constantly having to go all over the world, often at short notice. Likewise the Dental Centre offers full treatment for service personnel, though not for dependants who use local dentists. Pregnant mothers and their children, however, are treated at Lyneham.

The fuselage of the Comet being transported through Wootton Bassett for rebuild and siting at the Lyneham main gate.

Beyond the Medical Centre, the main way into the Lyneham complex is by what is called Pegasus Road. This thoroughfare is a clearway and, apart from not parking on it, speeds must not exceed 30mph, which is the limit throughout the station. This gives the base an unhurried though purposeful look. The system is equally well supervised. Every vehicle must either be registered or carry a pass, must keep to the traffic flow plan and only park in authorised areas well away from buildings. All are watched over by the RAF Police Flight strategically sited halfway along Pegasus Road. Lining the road are the NAAFI stores and Wessex Restaurant, the Sergeants Mess and the Gymnasium. A turning off Pegasus Road leads round the base to far sites that will be covered later in this chapter. Straight ahead are the wings, squadrons, flights and sections which collectively – like the intricate parts of a watch – make Lyneham tick.

Most first-time visitors to the base, especially those who are about to become air passengers, are taken directly to Operations Wing Headquarters. All flight arrangements are made in this building adjoining the airfield. Other buildings beside and behind it are concerned with the multiple tasks of training, servicing, supplying, loading and the hundreds of other duties necessary before a single aircraft leaves Lyneham. The passengers do not see this. They step from their coaches outside the terminal building, enter by the main doors and proceed along a wide corridor to the departure lounge.

In this day and age, most people have seen various departure lounges. The magnificent one at British Airways Terminal 4 Heathrow can be called state-of-the-art. That at RAF Lyneham reflects a more utilitarian service environment. The same facilities as those at London's

airports are there: chairs, refreshments, washrooms, customs and excise – only none of this is glamorized. This is because the Air Force is not a profit-making organisation. It works strictly to budgets most of which go into aircraft purchasing, crew training and maintaining services that are expensive enough. Notwithstanding, Lyneham has something not found in the impersonal airports of the world. Its personnel are friendly and helpful. Courtesy goes hand-in-hand with efficiency. No-one at Lyneham needs a course in public relations. It is already there and practised daily.

While the latest Lyneham passengers are being looked after, service wives are soothed and babies comforted, as VIPs are escorted without overmuch ostentation, the real work of the Operations Wing is taking place upstairs. Above their heads are the Task and Flight Planning Sections, the Meteorological Office, the Operations Room and a host of other essential inputs. Tasks are built round service requirements and aircraft availability. Crews in Flight Planning study weather conditions and airfield layouts on the other side of the world. The Met Office juggles with variable elements. The Ops Room is in contact with every Lyneham Hercules. Everywhere. Later more will be told of these vital activities.

Adjacent to the passenger terminal with Operations Wing HQ above it are hangars for the UK Mobile Air Movements Squadron (UK MAMS). This squadron has two main duties. First it is responsible for passengers and freight passing through RAF Lyneham. Taking an average month, squadron personnel look after some 5000 passengers and 1500 tons of freight. To handle these, a round-the-clock shift system is operated. Moreover, apart from UK passengers, overseas visitors have become so frequent at Lyneham the squadron runs a Foreign Section. This looks after aircraft, crews and their freight from as far afield as New Zealand and South America. The second squadron task is providing mobile teams to go anywhere at any time. Many of the places they go to have no organisation dealing with air movement activities. In fact some are extremely primitive. Yet UK MAMS teams, each consisting of six specialists – trained to cope in bad conditions over extended periods – have literally performed miracles of logistics.

Working alongside UK MAMS is No.47 Air Despatch Squadron which specialises in the preparation of stores for air dropping. The unit belongs to the Army's famed Royal Corps of Transport and is based permanently at Lyneham. The particular skill of No.47 Air Despatch Squadron is to assemble supply loads on to pallets for air dropping. The personnel

The Sergeants Mess has a membership of over 900 Senior NCOs plus civilians totalling around 1000.

The latest Lyneham accommodation for Junior Ranks is more like executive-style private housing.

concerned often fly with the Hercules crews and complete the drop. Their many duties include the heavy dropping of vehicles and resupply of petrol, oil, lubricants, food and other requirements needed by ground personnel or even those at sea.

The passenger departure doors from the terminal building lead directly on to the aircraft parking area of Lyneham airfield. There, as if eager for the next tasks, are the Hercules aircraft in their service colours, blue/red roundels, numbers on nose and tailfin, also red and white propeller blade tips. To be seen from the parking area are three large hangars in which aircraft servicing takes place, a function performed by the station's Engineering Wing. A description of this wing's activities later in the book will show the considerable technical expertise and experience background required to keep each Hercules airworthy.

Tucked behind these hangars are the headquarters of Nos 24 and 30 squadrons for flying the Hercules. The two other flying squadrons, No.47 and No.70, are on 'C' site further round the airfield. All four flying squadrons based at Lyneham are employed in the air transport role – that is, the carriage of passengers and freight around the globe – but each pair of squadrons have specialist roles. Nos 24 and 30 specialise in air tanking while Nos 47 and 70 are trained to carry out the full range of air dropping tasks. In addition however, all four squadrons are capable of receiving fuel in the air. At Lyneham no one says 'This is not my job'. Instead it is a place dedicated to positive thinking.

The Operations Wing, passenger and freight handling buildings, also the servicing hangars

The 'pan' or parking area for Lyneham's fleet of 61 Hercules is adjacent to the Air Terminal building.

Rare view of RAF Lyneham Air Terminal without several Hercules parked in front of it.

Air Traffic Control, Lyneham overlooking the runways with radar room beneath the tower.

and the two flying squadrons (Nos 24 and 30) are grouped around the top left of Pegasus Road. To the right, as one drives from the main gate, is a large office block, then a collection of other buildings between roads and car parks. As Lyneham contains so many buildings, only the main and most conspicuous ones are described here. The large office block serves as headquarters for another wing as important as Operations and Engineering. It houses the station's Administration Wing without whose services all activities would soon come to a standstill. These include accounting, ordering, catering, education, leaves, pensions and accommodation, to quote only a few.

For example, nearby is the Education Centre together with a full-scale lending library. Numerous Lyneham personnel have taken advantage of these facilities to further their education up to and including university degree standard. Many more make use of the fine library. As an added convenience, the Education Centre and library are next to a High Street bank (Lloyds) and a GPO Sub-Post Office. These amenities are conveniently placed for personnel working in the main central site and augment similar facilities in nearby Lyneham village.

Not far from the Education Centre is the station's Photographic Section responsible for most of the superb pictures in this book. Photographic personnel cover the spectrum of Lyneham activities from airborne assignments to social functions. Adjacent to this section are the flight simulators which come under No.242 Operational Conversion Unit. These electronic marvels, housed in specially constructed buildings, are programmed to create the condition one would (or could) encounter at the controls of the Hercules. Nearby are lecture rooms for training air and ground crews on Hercules minutiae, also electronic servicing workshops so necessary for present day aircraft.

The main central site at RAF Lyneham contains several other varied though equally necessary units. There are the Flying Clothing Stores (FCS) stocked with gear to cover conditions and environments that range from tropical to arctic. There is a fully functional hotel to help with accommodation of personnel in transit and the very important Flight Catering Unit (FCU). There is a section responsible for air publications and other vital documentation. Publications have to be kept strictly up to date and, just as strictly, read by all concerned. Moreover, the recipients reading them have to sign to the effect that they have done so. Then there is the RAF Regiment whose responsibilities include the defence training of all service personnel at Lyneham. There are guard dogs for patrol work and a gun practice range for obvious reasons. Security is maintained by frequent checks and trial infiltrations at all hours of the day and night.

Although the main site is both spacious and well laid out with grass areas and car parks, it only occupies a minor part of the total station. Beyond stretches the airfield proper with other sites dispersed round its periphery. A turning off Pegasus Road leads to these other sites. It passes the aircraft parking area outside the Operations Wing, on which are lined the Hercules fleet. One moment all is quiet until suddenly engines roar into life. An aircraft begins to make its way towards the airfield. Another which has just landed approaches the terminal building. Along the road by the tarmac, notices warn drivers about back wash from the propellers. Careless motorists could unexpectedly find themselves on the other side of the roadway.

Unexpectedly also, the road becomes part of the airfield – open, uncluttered and extending to the far distance. It is no longer possible to visualise the station layout as at the main site. The runways are too long, the subsidiary sites too dispersed. Another dimension is needed, that from the air as viewed daily by Hercules crews. Taking off from the main runways south-westwards into the prevailing wind, followed by climbing and banking, brings the layout together. To the north are the railway lines with the motorway between them. To the north-east stretches the conurbation of Swindon. Below, flattened when seen from the air, are the hills and woods, villages and roads surrounding RAF Lyneham.

Most prominent is the main runway, 7800 ft in length. It is designated 07/25 after its

31

Typical ground scene around Lyneham station showing hangars in which Hercules aircraft are maintained.

compass bearing and it has Instrument Landing System (ILS) facilities. The secondary runway (18/36) is 6000 ft long and is noteworthy because of a slight bend in the middle. One suspects that it was laid from each end thus accounting for the kink that Hercules pilots know only too well. A third, 4800 ft runway (13/31) is 'disused' meaning not utilised for take-offs and landings. Aircraft, however require plenty of room on the ground as well as in the air. They therefore taxi along sections of the third runway, and use the north-east end for compass swinging.

From the air it will be seen that the extremities of the runways are connected by a perimeter road just within the airfield boundaries. Around this road are six Crash Gates (CGs) so that, should an aircraft come down outside the base, fire engines and ambulances can reach the location in the swiftest possible time. Crash teams are on permanent duty, day and night, because Lyneham operations continue round the clock. Fortunately their services are not required for years on end. Again, as with security, crash teams are tested when they least expect it.

Lyneham and Bradenstoke villages, lie just outside the perimeter fence. Four other sites are ranged round the perimeter as follows. 'A' Site to the north is occupied by part of the Motor Transport Servicing (MTS) Squadron. 'C' Site to the south contains Motor Transport Control (MTC) and a Vehicle Training and Licensing (TAL) section. Heavy specialist vehicles – refuellers and cranes – operate from 'D' Site near the Air Traffic Control (ATC) tower. These various sites and services are necessary to accommodate over 300 vehicles in and around the station. It should also be mentioned that there is a well-equipped motor servicing centre located on the main site. This was organised, among other Lyneham amenities, so that service personnel could maintain their own vehicles, also purchase spare parts at discount prices.

Coverage of motor transport activities has entailed referring to 'A', to 'C' and 'D' Sites. Turning to 'B' Site, located south-east of the base across the Lyneham-Calne Road, this site fits unobtrusively between two large married quarters estates. 'B' Site has three hangars on it. Two contain bulk stores, such as furniture and office equipment, for use around the station. The third hangar is the headquarters and incorporates the workshops of 47 (Air Despatch) Squadron, Royal Corps of Transport. The hangar space and facilities are used for preparing pallet loads that are then taken across to their designated aircraft.

Along the south side of the base there is a small village named New Zealand. This community lies cheek by jowl with 'C' Site where several more important units are located. To begin with, Nos 47 and 70 flying squadrons (as distinct from 47(AD) Squadron RCT above) have their headquarters here. Nos 47 and 70 specialise in air drops as well as route operations. Here also are the Hercules Servicing School (HSS), two hangars for the Aircraft Engineering Squadron (AES), the Support Training Squadron (STS) and Motor Transport Control (MTC) as previously mentioned.

Fuel required for resident Hercules and other aircraft using the base comes to 'C' Site. Lyneham uses more than a million gallons of fuel a month. This is conveyed by underground pipeline from the supplier direct to 'C' Site. The arrangement avoids an endless stream of fuel tankers arriving by road. RAF tankers then take fuel to aircraft as required. 'C' Site also has a bay for handling liquid oxygen (LOX) needed on every aircraft.

After 'C' Site, the perimeter road loops under the southern extremity of the secondary

Typical aerial sight above Lyneham. Here three Hercules practise formation flying.

runway and continues up to 'D' Site. The most noticeable building on this site is Air Traffic Control (ATC) with its glass-topped upper storey and radar room below it noting every aircraft within a 40 mile radius of Lyneham. Like so many other key units at the base, Air Traffic Control is permanently manned, the word 'manned' including a high proportion of WRAF personnel. Right next to the control tower there is a bay where a Crash Team is always on duty. Behind the tower are two hangars allocated to the Fuel Tanker Pool and Propulsion Repair Flight.

Proceeding round the perimeter road, there is another loop to clear the south-western end of the main runway. At all these intersections one encounters sets of large warning lamps. The red/green lights are there to halt motor vehicles when aircraft are taking-off, landing and taxying. The perimeter road system also incorporates passing sections and dispersal areas, quick exit routes to the crash gates and standing water supply (SWS) hydrants. Once past Bradenstoke Village and 'A' Site, one arrives back at the north-eastern end of the main runway. As this is the usual aircraft landing end, a 3000 ft long pattern of white approach lights helps guide aircraft to the runway and is useful in bad weather.

Thus the airborne Hercules will approach Lyneham from the same direction as a first-time visitor arriving by road. Just as the visitor uses the road from Wootton Bassett to Lyneham Village, so the Hercules pilot follows the road and passes between the two Tockenhams below him. From aloft the fair county of Wiltshire, a mix of ancient and modern, stretches away on all sides – north to the Cotswolds, south to the Downs, ahead to the Bristol Channel. This is the fair sight that greets tired crews on their return from long route flying, from helping to alleviate famines and disasters, from a real war at the underside of the world. The same sight is there every day, seemingly unchanging apart from yearly seasons and ever-variable weather conditions. Yet, as this chapter has tried to show, the place is continually altering and adapting. How Lyneham progressed from the Stone Age to the Aviation Age is covered in the following chapter.

Chapter 3
HISTORICAL BACKGROUND

Lyneham is steeped in history both ancient and modern. Stone Age people once roamed this upland overlooking the Wiltshire Avon. Later there were small settlements. The Romans came and went. Vikings and Danes raided the area. By the time the Normans conquered Britain the main community was Bradenstoke now on the north side of the airfield. Lyneham, while not yet known as such, was probably included in the Domesday Book under the holding of Stoche. In those days the district was well wooded by Bradon Forest. The Earl of Salisbury founded an Augustinian Abbey at Bradenstoke in 1142 and historically the first time Lyneham itself is recorded was in 1224. In 1285 it was called Linham then Lynham by 1291 meaning a place where flax is grown.

The abbey at Bradenstoke went into decline from 1529 onwards following the Dissolution of the Monasteries. Up until the late 1920s the buildings were in quite good condition until William Randolph Hearst the American newspaper millionaire bought the site for its stone. Now little is left above ground apart from various ruins and the tower. In fact, if one knows where to look, the remains of the once great abbey are more recognisable from the air. As for nearby Lyneham, the village formed part of a manor in 1557 and remained so until the present century, quietly unaware of its destiny as a major air base.

Little is know about the population of Lyneham until 1810 when there were 833 people registered in the village and district. By 1841, there were 1317 parishioners including 179 labourers employed in laying the line for the nearby Great Western Railway. For some reason the population declined until 1921 when it was back to 835. As for Lyneham Church, now so much part of village and air station life, there have been buildings of worship since 1182. After the Dissolution, the church living became a curacy and around 1868 was promoted to a vicarage. In 1960, an agreement was reached, between the Bishop of Salisbury

Across the airfield from Lyneham is ancient Bradenstoke and the ruins of a medieval abbey. All that remains is part of the crypt, and the bell tower shown. (author photo)

Once the original guardroom was by Bradenstoke lane, but now it lies well within the much expanded air base.

and the Chaplain-in-Chief of the Royal Air Force, whereby RAF Chaplains were to serve the churches of Lyneham and Bradenstoke. Thus the two present day villages, one on each side of the airfield, remain historically intertwined.

So much for ancient history. This chapter is about Lyneham's modern history in general and aviation history in particular. During the late 1930s the Royal Air Force was more far-sighted than most. Locations all over the country were being assessed for various aviation requirements: fighter airfields, bomber bases, radar sites and maintenance units. The men from the Air Ministry made test diggings around Lyneham in 1937 and, though they went away, they did not forget. After the Munich Crisis in 1938, a large area was requisitioned and construction began. Building work to create and update RAF Lyneham has been going on ever since.

But let us move to the desperate days of 1940 when only the Royal Air Force stood between the nation's defeat or survival. The early grass airfield at Lyneham was to play a more humble role. The site would contain an aircraft storage unit. Hangars were built, all but two of which are still in use today. The unit's entrance was from the lane into Bradenstoke village. With hindsight, the storage programme was a most courageous one as the country was then daily facing the possibility of early defeat. To appreciate this last point, it should be mentioned that No.33 Maintenance Unit arrived at Lyneham on the 18 May 1940 – just as France was falling. Also, by September, when No.33 MU had accumulated a stock of 150 new aircraft of various types, the Battle of Britain was at its height.

The Luftwaffe paid two visits to Lyneham, the first on the 19 September killing four civilian workmen. However No.33 MU continued to build up stocks and those aircraft held at the time included Blenheims and Beaufighters, Wellingtons and Lysanders, as well as the famous Spitfires. During 1941, there were over 200 aircraft in storage at any one time. By

View of RAF Lyneham's oldest hangar built for World War II requirements and still in use.

September of that year, the unit had so many on its hands they occupied all available space at Lyneham. This curious situation was due to a shortage of pilots as flying training got under way and new squadrons were formed. So No.33 used surrounding sites, frequently in wooded areas to aid concealment.

The Maintenance Unit was not to remain the sole occupant of Lyneham airfield for much longer. On 16 August 1941, No.14 Service Flying Training School arrived from Cranfield and, three days later, control of the station passed from Maintenance to Flying Training Command which had authority over several other airfields in the area. At Lyneham, the advance training of pilots was carried out in Airspeed Oxfords known as Ox-Boxes. Training was intensive due to the war situation and many aircraft were written off with crew casualties. The graves of some can be seen in Lyneham churchyard. The Flying Training School was not long at Lyneham. It moved with its Ox-Boxes on the 20 January 1942 to be replaced by another unit – and another command.

The new unit was called Ferry Training and it came under the control of Ferry Command. Ferry Training's arrival on the 14th February 1942 (St. Valentine's Day) began Lyneham's association with long distance flying. The unit had British Wellingtons and Beauforts together with American Hudsons and Marylands. Then other flights converged on Lyneham: No.1442 with Blenheims, 1444 with Hudsons and 1445 with Liberators, also 1425 with more Liberators. The latter operated their Libs to the Mediterranean area carrying passengers and freight on the outward journey and returning with ferry crews. One aircraft took Mr Churchill to Cairo, then to Moscow. This was the first of several occasions when

Lyneham was privileged to operate Sir Winston Churchill's personal York aircraft on many wartime journeys.

the wartime Prime Minister used Lyneham aircraft which picked him up from other air-fields.

Wartime flights from England to the Mediterranean involved diversions and hazards. The Luftwaffe had bases in North-ern and Western France, also the Germans were active in the Iberian Peninsula. There-fore British ferry aircraft had to swing far out into the Bay of Biscay and indeed the Atlantic. This used much fuel and so aircraft departing from Lyne-ham would fill up at No.1 Overseas Unit at Portreath near to Redruth in Cornwall. Nevertheless many aircraft and crews were lost due to running out of fuel, mechanical failure or enemy action.

During the hectic year of 1942, what with various aircraft and crews at Lyneham engaged on training, ferrying and a host of other duties, a measure of order was introduced. In October, No. 1425 Communications Flight using Liberators was reconstituted as No.511 Squadron. Then in November Nos 1444 and 1445 Flights were amalgamated to form No.301 Ferry Training Unit. Most of the training was 'on-the-job'. The crews were screened by their instructors while engaged on wartime duties.

Meanwhile No.511 Squadron maintained regular Lyneham-Portreath-Gibraltar-Malta flights with Liberators. It also started mail services extending to Algeria and Libya using Albemarles. No.511 Squadron received the first of its twelve Albemarles early in November 1942 and lost one later that month. It crashed into the sea while taking off from Gibraltar. Another Albemarle did the same from Gibraltar a few months later.

Wartime Gibraltar was an ill-reputed air field. Apart from aircraft having to line up very carefully with a runway which extended into the sea at both ends, also having to take care of turbulence caused by southerly winds blowing over the Rock, arrivals were frequently greeted by fire from Spanish anti-aircraft guns. Fortunately these were not noted for accuracy. The vast number of aircraft movements from late 1942 onwards, however, seemed to have a disheartening effect on the gunners who eventually gave up in disgust. At least it reduced the hazard of an already complicated approach.

From early 1943, Lyneham was regularly used as the main terminal in Britain for passenger and freight flights by the British Overseas Airways Corporation. Service and civilian crews were to work side by side at Lyneham for the next two years. By then Lyneham had been provided with proper runways. Three were laid – two 6000 feet long and the third of 4800 feet.

The wartime work of No.33 Maintenance Unit at Lyneham must not be forgotten. This was a very active unit and its role kept changing to cope with service exigencies. No.33 MU became a Spitfire holding unit and by mid-1943 had some 250 Spitfires of various marks in storage. Then, from the end of 1943, it took on the extra task of assembling Hamilcar gliders using components built by outside firms. Over 70 were put together at Lyneham to be towed by heavy bombers such as Halifaxes and Stirlings for the invasion of France. Many were wrecked in France. Others lay around Lyneham for years to be used afterwards as storerooms and workshops. Considering they were made hurriedly and of wood, their working lives of over 30 years say much for wartime labour and materials.

But Lyneham was to have its share of wartime disasters as well as successes. On the 4th July 1943, one of No.511 Squadron's Liberators crashed at Gibraltar killing all aboard. It was carrying several VIPs including General Sikorski, the Polish Premier. Next, on the 10th August, one of 511's Albemarles was lost over the Spanish coast. Later that year the squadron began receiving newer aircraft better adapted to their responsibilities. They became the proud possessors of Avro Yorks and Douglas Dakotas for bread-and-butter Mediterranean routes. Better still, they received C-87 Liberators, specially modified from bomber versions, for trans-Atlantic and Far East routes.

Following the successful Normandy landings and breakthroughs of 1944, the rolling back of German forces during 1944/45, and preparations for the defeat of Japan, significant regroupings took place at Lyneham. In retrospect, it is heartening to note how the British aviation authorities, both military and civil, kept thinking well ahead. No. 511 Squadron was reformed with No. 246 to carry troops out to India and the Far East. In April 1945, the British Overseas Airways Corporation left Lyneham for a new London Airport then being made, at Heathrow. BOAC had, however, to use the old London Airport at Croydon for a time while the Heathrow runways and buildings were under construction.

It was a time of change everywhere including at Lyneham. A long range Meteorological Reconnaissance Flight No.1409, using Mosquito PR XVIs, arrived in October 1945 to be disbanded in May 1946. In poor weather on the 25th November 1945, a Stirling made an approach to Lyneham, missed the runway, and hit a group of buildings that including the Operations Room and a canteen. The Duty Operations Officer and a waitress in the canteen were killed, four others injured, the buildings and the aircraft destroyed, but the crew escaped.

For those who lived through the period, it was a restless part of their lives. The aviation authorities were literally juggling, grouping and regrouping. Fortunately at Lyneham the way ahead was becoming discernible. No.511 Squadron – the station's longest resident which had been re-formed with No.246 Squadron, flying Yorks – was to remain at Lyneham for the next ten and a half years. Two more squadrons were created for transport. Nos 99 and 206, formed on the 17th November 1947 and both flying Yorks, had time to settle in during 1947/48 because their busiest period ever was to hit them in the latter year.

By June 1948, relations with the Soviet Union had deteriorated to such a low point that all surface links between Western Germany and West Berlin were severed. There only remained the aerial link, but could that be maintained? By way of answering the question, all resources of British Transport Command were immediately placed at the disposal of the United States Air Force for the proposed Berlin Airlift. Nos 99, 206 and 511 Squadrons were detached from Lyneham to Wunstorf to take part in this vital operation.

The three Lyneham Squadrons flew throughout the airlift. They were joined at Wunstorf during July by No.242 Squadron, which was posted to Lyneham in the following year. The Yorks of these four RAF Squadrons contributed significantly to the 65,000 sorties carrying 400,000 tons of food, medicines and other supplies into the beleaguered city. It was a rigorous test for air and ground crews as well as aircraft. Such tremendous efforts could not be sustained without accidents, injuries and lives lost. The following are but a few of the losses:

Opposite right: Bristol Britannia crewed by Lyneham's No.99 Squadron flying over Mount Kilimanjaro, Tanzania in 1960.

On the 19th September 1948, MW288 of 206 Squadron lost an engine on take-off from Wunstorf and crashed killing all five crew members.

On the 10th October, MW305 of 99 Squadron overshot the runway when landing at Gatow and was written off, the crew escaping.

In November, MW270 of 206 Squadron landing at Wunstorf had to retract the undercarriage to prevent an overshoot. The crew was saved but not the aircraft.

In December, MW246 crashed on landing at Gatow and was totally destroyed.

These losses continued up to and even beyond the end of the airlift. No.99 Squadron lost another aircraft returning to London Northolt. In bad weather, the York collided with a Scandinavian Airlines DC-6. All seven people aboard the RAF aircraft MW248 were killed.

After the airlift, the four York Squadrons returned to Lyneham and Lyneham itself returned to a more measured pace of life. The Yorks, some of which had flown well beyond their allotted span, were phased out in the Autumn of 1949 and replaced by Hastings. These aircraft were to be the RAF's standard long-range transports for the next ten years until the arrival of its Britannias. Meanwhile, during 1951, No.511 Squadron carried troops to and from Korea and another Lyneham squadron evacuated British nationals from the Suez Canal zone. In 1953, many tons of sandbags were flown to the English East Coast when floods

Dramatic night scene of a Lyneham Britannia aircraft being prepared for a dawn take-off in 1959.

occurred. In 1954 No.511 Squadron mounted an airlift at Gibraltar to bring back survivors from the troopship *Empire Windrush* which had caught fire.

Although this history of Lyneham is abbreviated, the part played by the De Havilland Comet jet airlines must be stressed. After the disastrous series of accidents with the Comet 1 in civil service, the Government wished to inspire confidence in its replacement, the Comet 2. In other words, the RAF were to show the way. On the 17th June 1956, No.216 Squadron at Lyneham received the first Comet T2. This squadron was to operate two T2s and eight C2s safely and effectively. Less than a week later, the Secretary of State for Air was flown in a Lyneham Comet to Moscow. The following year, Her Majesty Queen Elizabeth II made her first flight in a Comet, also of No.216 Squadron. By 1957, RAF Comets were flying worldwide on routine operations.

Typical Lyneham activity in the early 1960s. Troops boarding Comet for overseas assignments.

The introduction of the Comet to Lyneham brought with it the need for a yet longer runway. To meet this, the main runway was extended to the north-east by nearly 2000 feet. This involved the demolition of two hangars which, while not directly in the path of the runway extension, were so close to it they may have formed an operational hazard.

The second post-war and non-piston engined aircraft to be operated from Lyneham was the Bristol Britannia. Nos 99 and 511 Squadrons shared twenty Britannias between them. With these Comets and Britannias, the Lyneham squadrons covered the RAF's long-range routes for the next ten years. The Comets were a great improvement over previous transport aircraft, being much faster and smoother fliers. They could reach Australia in a day and a half while a flight operation to and from mid-Pacific only took four days. For these reasons the Comets were much coveted as VIP aircraft. The Britannias also were quieter inside and out than the Hastings they replaced, and about 60 knots faster. Apart from ever-busy routine flying, Lyneham rose to the occasion at every emergency request. In July 1961, aircraft and crews helped carry the United Nations Peace-keeping Force into the Congo. Later the same year, Lyneham squadrons helped Kuwait.

Lyneham's involvement with Comets and Britannias continued throughout the sixties. Nos 99 and 511 Squadrons received extra Britannias, designated C2s. Then No.216 Squadron began getting Comet 4s with uprated Avon engines. This version carried 94 instead of 44 passengers at a higher speed over a longer range. In 1965, when Southern Rhodesia cut off the oil line to Zambia, Nos 99 and 511 Squadrons airlifted three and a half million gallons keeping up the operation well in to 1966.

During 1967 all three Lyneham Squadrons helped evacuate the British base at Aden, the operation going off without a hitch.

Mid-1967 brings us to an important change in the history of Lyneham. For the previous ten years, the station had been concerned with strategic transport. Now it commenced carrying out tactical duties. In order to play this part, a new and surprisingly useful aircraft would come to Lyneham. The aircraft was the Lockheed C-130 Hercules, the versatility of which is dealt with in the next chapter. No.36 Squadron moved to Lyneham on the 1st August 1967 to commence the transformation of the station to a tactical base starting with Hercules CMK1s.

That December saw the disbandment of Lyneham's first unit – No.33 Maintenance – which had been there since 1940. Through the years, No.33 MU steadily carried out its duties dealing with a wide range of aircraft including Meteors, Vampires, Canberras and Lightnings. One often-related Lyneham story involving No.33 MU, concerned an unfortunate Engineering

Line-up of Lyneham Comets in 1962; C2 'Taurus' in the foreground and three C4s in the background.

Comet C2 'Pegasus' landing at RAF Lyneham after a return ferry flight from the Far East.

43

Blackburn Beverley of
No.30 Squadron on
Middle East duty.

Officer. This individual, who was running up a Lightning, inadvertently became airborne. That aircraft was without a canopy and its 'pilot' wore no helmet, so he had no radio contact. To make a bad situation worse, the engineer was not strapped to the ejector seat. After several attempts, he managed to land the Lightning – a very creditable effort since his previous flying had been with Tiger Moths and gliders. That aircraft is now in the museum at Duxford. But getting back to the demise of No.33 Maintenance Unit, its type of work was no longer required. Thus, after 26½ years at Lyneham, the unit bowed out on the 31st December 1967.

February 1968 saw an increase in the Hercules strength at Lyneham when No.24 Squadron arrived with more of these aircraft to join No.36. These two squadrons were the forerunners of today's Lyneham Hercules Wing. Then No.511 Squadron moved twenty miles from Lyneham to Brize Norton. Like No.33 MU, No. 511 Squadron had spent many years at the station – 25 years and 2 months to be exact. Replacements came in the form of Nos 30 and 47 Squadrons from Fairford in February 1971 followed by No.48 Squadron from Singapore in September of the same year.

At this stage, that is in 1972/73, Lyneham had five squadrons flying Hercules aircraft in both strategic and tactical roles. Equal emphasis was placed on each role with much route flying and a great deal of support flying. What was then known as the Joint Airborne Task Force, involving 36 aircraft flying in formation, was exercised in Turkey during 1973 and in Germany in 1974. Although these were peacetime exercises, all flying and multi-task operations have their hazards. The German one gave rise to a disaster when strong wind shear caused ten paratroopers to drop and drown in the Kiel Canal. Another exercise in

44

Group Captain Leonard
Cheshire in a
Lockheed Hercules,
photographed in 1970.
Lyneham is an active
supporter of the
Cheshire Homes.

Lyneham Hercules over
the mountain Kingdom
of Nepal during the
famine relief operations
of 1973.

Italy had a further unfortunate outcome. One aircraft flew into the sea at night with a load of paratroops on board. A third fatal accident connected with a Lyneham Hercules occurred on the 10th September 1973. This aircraft was being used for pilot training. An engine had been closed down on take-off – a normal training procedure – when the other engine on the same side flamed out. It caused the aircraft to crash in woods near Colerne airfield 12 miles southwest of Lyneham killing all the crew. Two of them, Sergeant P.R. Coate and Master Air Loadmaster W.C. Nutt are buried in the graveyard of Lyneham church.

These disasters are mentioned to show the dark side of the aviation coin. Fortunately the bright side is inspiring; also, it must be stressed, thousands of successful operations are carried out as routine compared with the few which end in tragedy. In fact Lyneham has again and again turned potential tragedies into successes. For example, shortly after arriving at Lyneham, the CO of No.47 Squadron and his crew were diverted from a routine task to evacuate 450 people in Pakistan. During 1973, Lyneham squadrons helped airdrop food supplies to the remote regions of Nepal. In 1974, they repeated the exercise, that time in Senegal and Mali. On both occasions, the preparation and handling of food supplies was carried out by 47 Air Despatch Squadron, Royal Corps of Transport. This unit, now known as No.47 Squadron RCT, is still at Lyneham performing similar tasks on all sorties that involve the dropping of stores.

Early in 1974, the United Kingdom Mobile Air Movements Squadron (UK MAMS) came to Lyneham. This wonderfully adaptive organisation is responsible for the loading and unloading of freight, and also for passenger handling. It supplies teams to travel with aircraft and carries out its duties whenever and wherever required. The concept was proved in mid-1974 when the whole of Lyneham became involved in mass evacuations from Cyprus, as a result of the emergency which arose when the Turkish and Greek forces came into conflict. Lyneham Comets and Hercules squadrons became responsible for evacuating civilians of many nationalities as well as service personnel and their dependents. Over 8000 people were flown from Akrotiri to Lyneham in a copybook operation.

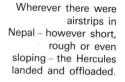
Wherever there were airstrips in Nepal – however short, rough or even sloping – the Hercules landed and offloaded.

One consequence of the unrest in Cyprus was the posting of No.70 Squadron, also flying Hercules, from Akrotiri to Lyneham where it has remained ever since. The move, together with subsequent groupings and re-groupings, resulted in the Hercules force being concentrated at Lyneham. All these changes took place amid emergency calls and routine work. There were calls for Lyneham to help in Nicaragua, Australia, Turkey, Italy and India when various disasters struck. There was the ever-present support for British service personnel, which included the Army and Royal Navy, also the commitment to NATO. And there was the Falkland War.

When Argentina invaded the Falkland Islands on the 2nd April 1982, the British Armed Forces had an 'instant war' on their hands. Less than 24 hours after the invasion, the first Hercules aircraft left Lyneham for Wideawake Airfield on Ascension Island.

It carried a six-man team from the Mobile Air Movements Squadron. This unit would have the awesome responsibility of handling loads sufficient to support the Task Force making its way to the South Atlantic. During the following three months, dozens of Hercules flights were made between Lyneham and Ascension carrying more than a million pounds of supplies per week.

By the middle of April, a fully loaded Hercules was taking off from Lyneham every four hours. Every service person at the base and many more civilians worked flat out to maintain the effort. The heavily laden Hercules landed en route, either at Gibraltar or Dakar, to refuel. The average flying time from Lyneham to Ascension was 14 hours.

But Ascension was still 3400 miles from the Falklands. The Task Force needed supplies

Hercules 182 prepares to air drop 1 ton of grain contained in 87 lb sacks secured to baseboards.

as it continued southwards. Therefore the Hercules range had to be extended: the Engineering Wing at Lyneham was already working on this problem. The immediate solution was to fit air-to-air refuelling probes on Hercules freighters so that they could be topped up by Victor tankers. Simultaneously a programme was launched to install long-range fuel tanks in the freight bays of other Hercules. The initial aircraft had two extra tanks and subsequent aircraft four, each tank containing 7000 lb of fuel. The aircraft had hose drums installed on their loading ramps, the hose being trailed through a slot cut in the ramp.

The first Falklands long range flight, with refuelling from a Victor, was made on the 16th May when a No.47 Squadron Hercules dropped paratroops and stores. By the time the aircraft returned to Ascension, it had clocked up 24 hours and 5 minutes flying time. These long range Hercules flights, sustained by air-to-air refuelling, continued throughout the conflict. By the 3rd June, the Lyneham fleet had exceeded 10,000 flying hours. On the 24th June, the first Lyneham Hercules touched down at liberated Stanley. It was followed the next day by another Hercules returning Mr Rex Hunt, the island's Governor, back from his enforced exile. On the 28th June, a Lyneham Hercules was unable to land at Stanley because of the weather and returned to Ascension. It achieved this by repeated flight refuelling and in the event set up a world endurance record for the Hercules of 28 hours 4 minutes.

Margaret Thatcher, as Leader of the Opposition, visits Lyneham. Later, as Prime Minister, she flew to Port Stanley in a Lyneham Hercules.

The Hercules that flew more than 1 million pounds of relief supplies into war torn Kampuchea.

Early stage of South Atlantic operations – a Victor tanker refuels a Hercules. Soon Hercules refuelled Hercules.

Scene over the Falklands. A Hercules tanker with four Phantoms and air-to-air refuelling hose extended. (Phil Fox)

Once the islands had been retaken, priority was given to having an air defence system capable of defeating any future threat. Harrier GR's and Rapier missiles deployed during the conflict were retained, and a squadron of Phantoms flown out to the islands. To provide flight refuelling capabilities, Lyneham air and ground crews for the Hercules tanker aircraft were detached to the Falklands as No.1312 Flight. Later the Harriers were withdrawn but the Phantoms and Hercules tankers remained. To maintain them, Lyneham crews on detachment

Archive picture of Hercules with its port wing tip damaged while operating in the Falklands.

served tours of four months. Apart from these tanker activities, all Lyneham squadrons flew freight to Stanley until the new airfield – capable of accepting British Airways 747s and RAF Tristars – was completed. Today these remote but still British islands are served each week by RAF Tristars and, until March 1989, by Lyneham Hercules.

Throughout the eighties, Lyneham Hercules aircraft have continued to provide much needed routine and emergency support. During 1983, Hercules assisted United Nations Peace Keeping Forces. During March 1984, the ever-ready Hercules delivered large quantities of relief supplies, including lorries, to Upper Volta. In early November of that year came the terrible famine disaster in Central and Northern Ethiopia. On the 4th November, six Lyneham Hercules arrived at Addis Adaba with men and equipment to set up a detachment for relief operations. Relief work began next day with grain airlifted and delivered to rough strips in the drought stricken areas. The strips were situated at up to 9000 feet above sea level, moreover their surfaces were very rough and some were even sloping. These hazards, combined with the high temperatures and heavy loads, made for difficult and demanding operations. Aircraft tyres were soon worn smooth while stones, flung up during take-off and landing, punctured the undersides of many aircraft.

Yet Ethiopian relief was maintained month after month. From February 1985 onwards, Nos 24 and 30 Squadron crews were engaged on airland relief work while Nos 47 and 70 Squadrons specialised in airdropping over remote areas. When the Ethiopian exercise ended in November 1985, more than 32,000 tonnes of supplies had been delivered by the Lyneham Hercules of which 18,000 tonnes were landed and 14,000 dropped. Since then, RAF Lyneham and its Hercules have continued to live up to the Station's motto of 'Support, Save and Supply'.

Each year, month, week and, indeed, every day, sorties are taking place. These are usually routine, yet the need for reacting to emergencies is ever-present. Following Ethiopia, there were more relief operations in Mexico and Columbia, search and rescue requirements in many parts of the world, together with support duties for British forces whenever these are moved and wherever they are posted. Which brings us to present day Lyneham.

The mainstay of the station consists of four Hercules Squadrons: Nos 24 and 30, 47 and 70. The four squadrons at Lyneham are employed in the Air Transport Role and, to this end, share the same planes. The squadrons, however, are paired for other activities. While all are engaged on route flying, Nos 24 and 30 Squadrons also specialise in airborne tanking, while Nos 47 and 70 Squadrons are experts in air dropping supplies, equipment and paratroops. Working closely with these four squadrons are No.242 Operation Conversion Unit, the United Kingdom Mobile Air Movements Squadron, No.47 Air Despatch Squadron and, of course, station support staff such as the Operations and Engineering Wings.

No.242 Operational Conversion Unit, providing a continuous training programme, is responsible for the training of all newcomers to the Hercules fleet, also for further courses to maintain efficiency and to learn the latest techniques.

Newcomers who arrive at Lyneham after completing their basic flying training attend Ground Training School. This, as the name suggests, provides ground instruction on the Hercules aircraft - its design, construction, systems and performance. The new crews then pass on to simulator training, which covers cockpit drills, normal and emergency procedures. Each simulator contains a complete flight deck and can reproduce any airborne situation including a visual display of the ground over which the aircraft is 'flying'.

Hercules lands on a rough air strip in drought stricken area of Ethiopia during this 14 month Lyneham mission. (Graphique)

51

After simulator training, would-be Hercules crews progress with the conversion squadron to flying aircraft. Thereafter, although a limited amount of informal training is carried out by the operational squadrons, the operations themselves naturally take priority. The crews therefore are required to return to No.242 OCU once a year for two-week refresher courses to make sure that optimum flying standards are maintained. Another of the OCU's responsibilities is to convert selected crews for specific Hercules duties such as tanking, air refuelling and various forms of transport support. No.242 OCU also provides training to crews from many other Air Forces operating a variety of C-130 models.

Summing up, the history of RAF Lyneham is one of an ancient site which, in the last 50 years, has grown from a wartime maintenance unit to the RAF's principal air transport base and, of course, home of Britain's Hercules fleet. Lyneham is known to Service Personnel the world over as a major terminal for long-distance trooping flights. Thousands of men, women and children have flown from Lyneham airfield or returned to it at all hours of the day and night. Lyneham never closes, is never silent or still. It operates round the clock, seven days a week, 365 days a year. Lyneham's uniformed and civilian personnel exceeds 3000. Adding dependants, this increases the Lyneham team to well over 10,000 people. Their collective efforts revolve round a remarkable aircraft, the subject of the next chapter: the Lockheed C-130 Hercules.

Chapter 4
HERCULEAN ANATOMY

It is always interesting to hear people's comments on seeing the Hercules aircraft for the first time. They tend to stare somewhat disbelievingly and the first words they use include 'squat, strong, purposeful'. Those who know more about the Hercules would say the aircraft is deceptive, though in the nicest sense of the word. For the Hercules is deceptively agile, capable and versatile. The aircraft is rightly named because, like the Greek God, it cheerfully tackles an ever-increasing and never-ending series of labours. Some may find difficulty in coming to love a mere machine, but those who know the Hercules and what it can do for them are full of admiration. Much has been written about the Hercules so this chapter is more of an introduction to the basic aircraft and the RAF version used at Lyneham.

How did the Hercules come into being? Like every other aircraft, there was a need. Unlike many aircraft, however, the Hercules has gone far beyond original expectations. The requirement arose around 1950 after it had taken the Americans six weeks to move two army divisions to Korea. The Pentagon planners wanted a machine capable of transporting troops, their supplies and equipment to any part of the world, then to land on the roughest of airstrips. As one nameless colonel remarked: 'Hell, we need a medium transport that can land on unimproved ground, be extremely rugged, be primarily for freight, with troop-carrying capability, and carry about 30,000 pounds over a range of 1,500 miles.'

Lockheed and the Hercules were going to do a great deal better than that.

But first came the GOR and the RFP, acronyms for General Operational Requirement and Request for Proposal. The GOR was issued by the US Air Force on the 21st February 1951 and this was closely followed by the RFP which went to Boeing, Douglas, Fairchild and Lockheed. Each company had foreseen the need and begun advance work on their responses. The US authorities were equally active because, within five months, Lockheed was awarded a contract to build two prototypes of its winning concept designated YC-130.

In the aviation industry, the Lockheed Corporation is well known for producing some of the world's most innovative and amazing aircraft. From Lockheed have come the P-38 twin-boom World War II fighter, the U-2 high flying spy plane, the L-1011 TriStar airliner jet and the S-71 Blackbird, the World's highest-flying, fastest-cruising aircraft. Before arriving at the Hercules concept, Lockheed did its homework. It gathered all available information from the Pentagon at Washington DC, from Strategic Air Command headquarters in Nebraska, Andrews Air Force Base in Maryland and the US Army's Airborne Headquarters at Fort Bragg, North Carolina. Certain forecasters estimated that the ultimate production run could reach 2000 aircraft. Nearly 40 years later, Lockheed is nearing this figure.

During the preliminary stage, the aircraft specification grew more and more demanding. The US Army and Air Force wanted a fast, ocean-spanning airlifter to take 90

A C-130 Hercules flying over the Lockheed plant at Marietta, Georgia. (Courtesy Lockheed Aeronautical Systems)

troops over 2000 mile stages. The aircraft should be able to slow down to 125 knots for paratroop dropping and, as stressed over and over again, be able to land on hastily prepared strips. Once more, a nameless individual summed up the last requirement in a memorable phrase saying, 'It has to land in a mudhole'.

Lockheed's Advanced Design Department must have frowned over these mounting challenges. What the Customer wanted was a combination of jeep, truck and aeroplane. Ideas became drawings that were in turn converted to models. The requirement for a hold cargo floor at truck bed level entailed a low slung fuselage with a high wing. Thus the landing gear would have to be short and its main wheels tucked into the sides of the fuselage. The rear combined luggage door and loading ramp meant a high tail plane. At Lockheed's Burbank plant in California just about everyone who could make an intelligent suggestion was encouraged to comment. These were reduced to three essentials: simplicity, reliability and rugged construction. Regarding the first – simplicity – the aviation industry was not only surprised by the resultant aircraft configuration, but also by the many features that were radical for their time.

Unusual airframe design	Low level floor
Turboprop powerplants	Rear loading door
Greenhouse type nose	High-pressure hydraulics
Tall massive tailplane	High-voltage electrics
Short landing gear	Fully boosted servo controls
Cavernous cargo hold	Full fuselage pressurisation

54

Yet, despite innovations, the C-130 is a relatively simple plane of 75,000 parts. It certainly is reliable and rugged, purpose-built to tackle seemingly impossible missions as well as to last. The doughnut-shaped main wheel tyres, for example, placed tandem-wise at the base of the fuselage – as in a heavy truck – make landings and take-offs possible from very inferior airstrips. The upward sweep of the rear fuselage provides headroom for loading. The 23 windows round the nose give superb flight deck vision. As one UK aerospace designer asked, 'Why didn't we think of it?'

The first of the YC-130 prototypes from Lockheed's Burbank plant flew on the 23rd August 1954, using only 855 feet of runway. At the time, plans were underway for Lockheed to have a second plant at Marietta in Georgia where, among other aircraft, the Hercules would be mass produced. If all went well, a production run up to the projected 2000 aircraft might be achieved. The initial C-130 production aircraft rolled out of Marietta on the 10th March 1955 and, on the 7th April after passing all its ground tests, took off from a 10,000 ft runway. This time it began flying at the 800 ft mark and, by the end of the runway, the C-130 was 2500 feet up in the air. Lockheed's Chief Test Pilot said: 'In my twenty years of flying, I have never flown in an aircraft so easy to handle.'

Of course, there were teething troubles and for six months following the first flight, the Lockheed team literally worked flat out to ensure the aircraft test programme remained on schedule. Every problem that occurred was tackled there and then. To give only one but significant example, there was the occasion when the landing gear would not deploy and there had to be a belly landing. Some of the skin was torn off, but none of the airframe structure needed replacing. Nor did the high wing-mounted propellers. 'We patched it up', said the Lockheed engineers, 'and had the plane back on the flight test programme

The production line on which hundreds of Hercules in more than fifty versions have been assembled. (Courtesy Lockheed)

ten days later.' This was an early testimony to the ruggedness of the C-130.

An interesting aspect of their programme – particularly to the British aircraft industry – was ground-rig testing the C-130 fuselage for fatigue pressurisation effects. The Americans were doing this using hundreds of individual containers in the fuselage to minimise damage if there was an explosion. At that period, their British counterparts were battling with Comet 1 fatigue problems. The British developed the technique of testing in huge water tanks and Lockheed Marietta became the first US company to adopt the UK method with the Hercules, which was eventually tested to four times that of its anticipated operational life. Meanwhile, the air testing programme continued and, among other tests, the C-130 was subjected to 3g manoeuvres and rolling pull-ups at 60 degrees of bank.

The first service establishment to take delivery of Hercules was the 463rd Troop Carrier Wing of US Tactical Air Command. Five aircraft were delivered to Ardmore, Oklahoma on the 9th December 1956. As a matter of interest, this very first Hercules, named *City of Ardmore* took part in the 1981 Greenham Common Air Tattoo where it won the Concours D'Elegance against twenty other C-130s. Early Hercules exploits included the airlifting of troops to the Caribbean and Lebanon, the air transporting of supplies to the Arctic and Antarctic, Himalayas and Equatorial Africa. One famous exploit was the use of Hercules to rescue hostages held by terrorists at Entebbe Airport.

The Royal Air Force became a major user of the Hercules as a result of assessments and a decision reached in 1965 to order 66 of these aircraft. The C-130H version was chosen, though with changes as given in the next paragraph. Before that, however, it should be mentioned how the Hercules was progressively improved from the original C-130A to the C-130H. Incredibly, Lockheed increased the aircraft speed by 11 per cent, payload by 26 per cent and range by 52 per cent. At the same time, take-off distances when loaded were reduced by 17 per cent. The Hercules has remained basically simple while responding to many improvements.

The Lockheed C-130Hs for the RAF were designated C-130Ks because of the changes required. The main modifications included the installation of British radio, radar, autopilot and avionics, also UK roller and attachment equipment within the hold. The initial C-130K flew at Marietta on the 19th October 1966. Wearing RAF roundels, but otherwise unpainted, it came to Britain for adaptation by Marshall of Cambridge and finally full RAF camouflage livery. No.36 Squadron at Lyneham became the first to have Hercules aircraft and completed its re-equipment by September that year, when No.48 Squadron based at

An historic picture showing the first Hercules being built for the United Kingdom. (Courtesy Lockheed)

Singapore began to take deliveries. Other RAF squadrons to receive Hercules were No.70 at Akrotiri, and Nos 24, 30 and 47. Eventually, after various regroupings, the RAF's total Hercules fleet was operated by Nos 24, 30, 47 and 70 Squadrons all based at Lyneham.

The RAF now fly two versions of the C-130H/C-130K Hercules in CMK1 and CMK3 versions. The Lyneham Hercules CMK1s are the short or standard length models at 29.79 m (97 ft 9 in). The CMK3s are 37.37 m (112 ft 9 in) long, the stretched type having two fuselage sections or 'plugs' inserted fore and aft of the mainplane. Due to the presence and sheer size of the aircraft, it is not easy for a newcomer to differentiate between the standard and stretch versions. The best clue lies in the position of the three fuselage windows behind the port side crew door. If the windows are close to the door, that is the standard or short aircraft. If there is a noticeable distance between the door and the windows then that is the stretched version. The second section or plug aft of the mainplane is again difficult to distinguish. Together, however the 2.54 m (8 ft 4 in) forward plug and the 2.03 m (6 ft 8 in) one aft make significant differences such as:

7 cargo pallets instead of 5   or
4 vehicles and 4 trailers instead of 3 and 2   or
128 troops in transit instead of 93   or
92 paratroops instead of 64   or
97 stretcher cases instead of 74

Actually the CMK3, with its extra plugs but the same engines, will carry less weight than the CMK1. Where the CMK3 scores, however, is that it can accommodate more bulk because of the increased length to its hold. RAF Lyneham loadmasters have learned to turn these factors to wide-ranging advantage.

Above left: Roll-out of first Royal Air Force Hercules in the autumn of 1966. (Courtesy Lockheed)

Above: Hand-over of the first Hercules CMk1 by the US Air Force to the Royal Air Force. (Courtesy Lockheed)

Line-up of RAF Hercules at Marietta for programmed test flying and hand-over. (Courtesy Lockheed)

Thirty of the RAF Hercules were stretched, but a walk round either a CMK1 or a CMK3 version does not readily reveal the technical worth of this remarkable aircraft. Let us, therefore have a closer look at it. The fuselage itself is of near circular cross-section flattened at the bottom to provide the cargo hold floor. Crew access is through the port side crew door mentioned, a swing-down door with integral steps. There are two less prominent doors for paratroop dropping on each side of the fuselage to the rear of the main landing gear. More noticeable is the cargo hold access/exit arrangement at the rear. This is made up of a ramp which is lowered for roll-on/off operations and a door that rises into the roof thus providing generous top clearance. The number of doors (5) makes the fact of the

The CMk3 stretched Hercules is capable of taking longer loads due to fuselage plugs fore and aft of the mainplane.

A Hercules during manufacture showing the 'plugs' inserted to stretch a CMk1 into a CMk3. (Lockheed photo via Adrian Balch)

Hercules being fully pressurised and air-conditioned all the more impressive. Incidentally, out of the 23 flight deck windows, only two can be opened but all are designed to withstand a sledgehammer blow.

While walking round the Hercules, the low and somewhat unusual landing gear keeps attracting attention. It does so by its very unobtrusiveness. Although the gear is large and rugged, it is not easy to see even at close hand. The twin-wheel nose gear, steerable through 60 degrees on either side of centre, remains barely visible on the ground. As for the mains with their balloon-like low-pressure (80-100 psi) tyres, these are paired in tandem but

Hercules CMk1 rotating for take-off shows well the tandem main wheel and the twin nose gear.

The port main wheels, detailing the robust gear-doors.

half-hidden by fairings along the side of the lower fuselage. Nose wheel retraction is by conventional hydraulic actuator mechanism while the mains are raised, again hydraulically, via long-stroke screw jacks. Wheeltrack is 4.36 m (14 ft 2 in). The main landing gear wheels only are fitted with hydraulically-applied brakes, also anti-skid devices.

After walking round the Hercules aircraft, a first time viewer may well stand back and look up at the massive mainplane across the broad shoulders of the fuselage. It will be seen that the planform of the wing centre-section is rectangular while the outer sections are tapered towards the wing tips. The mainplane is of twin-spar construction and spans 40.57 m (132 ft 7 in). The ailerons are fitted with trim tabs and trailing edge flaps extend from the wing roots to the ailerons. The leading edge of the mainplane contains ducting for engine-bled hot air to provide anti-icing.

This brings us to the four Allison T56 turboprop engines driving four-bladed Hamilton Standard propellers 4.11 m (13 ft 6 in) in diameter. The T56 is a 14-stage axial flow engine with six combustion chambers. The propeller, driven through a reduction gearbox, is a constant-speed, fully feathering unit with reverse pitch. This last feature is extremely useful for normal landings, and vital for the many hair-raising exploits required of Hercules aircraft. There are eight fuel tanks: four built in mid-wing, two auxiliaries in the wing roots and an external pod-type tank suspended on each side between the engines. The four main tanks contain 8-9000 lb of fuel apiece, the two auxiliaries 6000 lb each and the two external tanks a further 9000 lb in each case. Maximum take-off fuel weight is 62,900 lb; or almost exactly 28 tons! The ground refuelling point is sited at the aft end of the starboard main landing gear fairing. All of the Lyneham Hercules are equipped for flight refuelling, the probe projecting from the flight deck roof slightly offset to starboard. Ground refuelling takes place at 6000 lb min. Fuel can be dumped through outlet valves at the tips of the mainplane.

The height of the Hercules tailplane is an impressive 11.70 m (38ft 3 in) measured from the ground to the tip of the fin. This is accentuated by the upward sweep of the rear fuselage to provide plenty of headroom in the freight loading area. The tail unit is an all-metal structure with the vertical fin containing three spars while the horizontal stabiliser is of two-spar

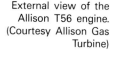

External view of the Allison T56 engine. (Courtesy Allison Gas Turbine)

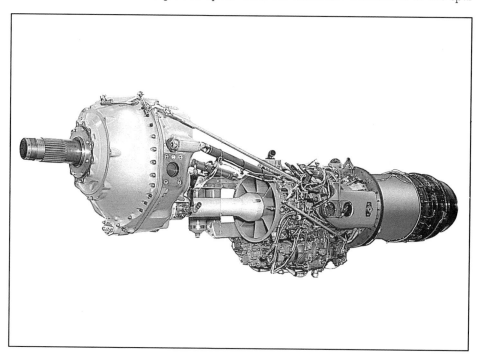

Assembly of the
Hamilton Standard
54H60 propeller for
Hercules powerplants.
(Courtesy United
Technologies)

construction. The hydraulically-operated rudder and elevators carry trim tabs. Anti-icing is effected by air bled from the engines and ducted to the tail. An anti-collision lamp is fitted at the top of the vertical fin. Two high frequency (HF) aerials run from three- quarters way up the tail to lead-in units in the roof aft of the flight deck. The tail fin is also fitted with an omni-range (VOR) aerial.

The Hercules at RAF Lyneham contain a wide range of radio, radar and avionics equipment. Apart from the two kinds of aerials mentioned, there are two pillar-type UHF fittings positioned above the flight deck and along the fuselage roof. Other items are contained in the aircraft envelope, notably the protuberant radome enclosing the radar scanner in the nose. One of the most distinct Hercules adaptations, based elsewhere, but often seen at Lyneham is the WMk2 version used for weather reconnaissance. The modifications include a 6.7 m (22 ft) long nose probe (with red and white stripes like an airborne barber's pole) and the scanner mechanism in a pod above the flight deck. This aircraft is affectionately known as 'Snoopy'.

Essential, though not so easy to visualise, are the various Hercules systems. Aircraft pressurisation and air-conditioning are provided by tapping the turbine engine compressors, the Flight Engineer having control responsibility for these two inter-related systems. He maintains sea level pressure up to 18,000 ft through to a final differential setting of 7.5 psi

at 33,000ft – ie, the cabin altitude is as at 8000ft. Regarding warmth, the heating system is capable of automatically sustaining an inside temperature of +70°F when the outside air temperature is as low as -65°F. At the other end of the scale, when outside air temperatures are in the region of 100°F, the Hercules interior can be cooled to around 80°F for crew and passenger comfort.

There are three independent hydraulic systems to 'flex the muscles' of the aircraft – named utility, booster and auxiliary. Hydraulic pumps sited beside Nos 1 and 2 port engines supply the utility system while pumps by Nos 3 and 4 starboard engines serve the booster system. Both systems operate at a working pressure of 210 kg/cm (3000 psi). The utility and booster systems are completely separate and cannot be interconnected. The utility system

Close-up of the Hercules' tailplane with rudder, trim tabs and aerial fittings.

supplies the flying controls plus flaps, landing gear, mainwheel brakes and nosewheel steering. The booster system supplies only the flying controls, though not by the same hydraulic lines. The auxiliary system, used for emergencies, is operated either electrically (through an electro-hydraulic pump unit) or by a hand pump.

As for the aircraft electrics, these are generated primarily by four engine-driven 40 k VA AC alternators plus another 40 k VA auxiliary unit. A gas turbine compressor unit (GTC) supplies air for a number of purposes including powering the fifth alternator driven from an air turbine motor (ATM). Where DC current is required, this is done through transformer rectifiers. On the ground the electrics, also heating and cooling air, are produced by means of the gas turbine unit which also supplies compressed air for engine starting. A 24 volt battery is also installed in a compartment beside the port side crew door for general ground requirements.

The most impressive way to enter the Hercules is via the rear cargo ramp, this opening made all the more spacious by the door panel retracted into the roof. The height of the Hercules cargo hold is 2.78 m (9 ft 1 in) and its width 3.085 m (10 ft 1 in) – that inch depends

Nose-on view of
Hercules showing radar
dome, air-to-air refuelling
probe and the 23 flight
deck windows.

Side view of the CMk1
Hercules which is the
standard or shorter
version for carrying
dense freight.

WARNING:
WITH CREW MEMBERS
ABOARD, THIS DOOR WILL
BE OPENED AND CLOSED
FROM THE INSIDE ONLY
TO OPEN-
TURN HANDLE AND
LET DOOR ROTATE DOWN

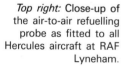

Top right: Close-up of the air-to-air refuelling probe as fitted to all Hercules aircraft at RAF Lyneham.

Above: Crew entrance door. Inside ahead are further steps up to the flight deck.

on whether the aircraft is a standard CMk1 or the stretched CMk3. In both cases, there are impressively roomy interiors. Looking along the hold, it is immediately apparent that the Hercules is a basic utilitarian aircraft and not one, as is an airliner, for cosseting people. No pleasing panels cover the bones of the airframe, no comforting upholstery pads the seats. Instead there is a bare metal floor, pierced or studded for various fitments, and gaunt mounting beams for troop seating or stretcher cases. Clipped round the walls are swing-down seats (that can and do serve as bunks), life jackets, oxygen bottles and masks, fire extinguishers, and water containers, toilets and urinals. Crowding the cabin ceiling are air ducts, hydraulic pipes and electrical leads. The overall impression is of a workaday no-nonsense aircraft with little concession for creature comforts.

On the port side of the forward cargo hold bulkhead – known as Bulkhead 245 for loading purposes – there is a doorway leading to the flight deck. A few steep steps take one up to a floor above the nose wheel bay. From this level the Hercules' 23 flight deck windows are seen to their full advantage. The C-130 pilot does not just have the meagre horizontal slot found on many planes, he enjoys wide lateral as well as up and down vision. He and his co-pilot can look well back to about 30 degrees aft and also see what is happening beneath.

An RAF Hercules air crew consists primarily of five members: captain, co-pilot, navigator, flight engineer and, that very important person on air-transport work, the loadmaster. Like everywhere else on this aircraft, the flight deck is a strictly functional rather than a comfortable cabin. The four seats are solidly built to last with only the canvas covered cushions showing signs of wear. Similarly the control and instrument panels facing, between and above the pilots are not masterpieces of ergonomic design. No smooth banks of touch switches and computer graphics meet the eye. Instead there is good, meaty engineering – levers to be pulled, wheels to be turned, big round dials to be watched. One can see where the additions and subtractions of equipment have taken place.

By convention, the captain occupies the left-hand seat and his co-pilot the right. Each has the usual control column and rudder bar arrangement, hydraulically coupled to the flying control surfaces, also access to the engine control levers on a floor-mounted console between the two seats. The flight engineer sits behind and between the pilots, thereby

The Hercules ramp
lowered to horizontal
truckbed level position
and rear door retracted
upwards into tail.

Interior of empty hold
revealing basic structure
and fittings such as
swing down canvas
benches.

Above: Same view looking forward along port side of well netted and tensioned freight filling the hold.

Above right: The hold side door is primarily used for paratroop dropping; it is also convenient during loading operations.

Facing page: The captain's seat on the Hercules flight deck. The wheel to the left of the control column is for steering during taxying.

overseeing all panels. The navigator has a desk and instrumentation of his own behind the co-pilot next to a pair of wall-mounted crew rest bunks. For crew sustenance, there is a galley at the top of the flight deck entry steps where rations can be heated. None of these amenities are luxurious. In fact they are decidedly spartan.

Facing the captain is the main flight panel with all essential instrumentation: altimeter (ALT), attitude direction (ADI), airspeed (ASI), turn and slip (TSI), horizontal situation (HSI) and vertical speed (VSI). These key indicators have standby units elsewhere on the flight deck. The horizontal situation indicator (a sophisticated compass) can have signals from ground navigation beacons fed into it as selected by the pilot. Another flying aid is the radar scanner that can look from 15 degrees down to 15 degrees up, both relative to the aircraft axis, over 10-175 mile distances. This is especially useful when flying in heavy cloud because, apart from detecting other aircraft, it can give warning of cloud turbulence a long way ahead. The navigator has an equivalent screen. Both are also used for mapping as the scanner shows coastlines, lakes and even ships. The primary ground-based navigation aids fitted include two VHF omni-range (VOR) units for bearing only, two tactical air navigation (TACAN) units for range and bearing, and one automatic directing finding (ADF) unit again for bearing only. Each unit has readouts at three positions, for the captain, co-pilot and navigator.

The centre front panel is taken up with engine instrumentation. Running conditions of the Allison T56s are registered on dials four to a row so that comparisons as well as individual readings can be made. Heading this panel are the torquemeters. As each engine swings a large diameter propeller, torque is a major flight consideration. The next two rows of

The co-pilot's seat. The co-pilot duplicates the captain's main functions and is responsible for flap and landing gear operations.

dials are concerned with engine rpm and turbine inlet temperatures. Next there are gauges for fuel flow which on the Hercules amounts to 2400 lb/hour per engine at take-off dropping to 1250 lb/hour at economic cruising. The fifth, sixth and seventh rows cover the essential parameters of oil temperature, pressure and quantity. These temperatures are controlled between 60-85 C, pressures run at 50-60 psi and quantities should be 8-10 US gallons.

The co-pilot's panel duplicates the primary flying instruments such as ALT, ADI, ASI, TSI, HSI and VSI while covering certain functions other than those handled by the captain. These include flap positioning and landing gear selection. Flap positioning on the Hercules is 50 per cent for take-off and 100 per cent for landing. Other settings are required for special requirements like air drops. The signalling of landing gear position is simple and straightforward as befits the Hercules: when the gear is up, the indicators say UP.

Ranged round the sides of the captain and co-pilot are further units, panels, gauges and controls. The captain has a VHF/UHF radio for all air traffic, civil as well as military, while the co-pilot has a UHF set mainly for military traffic. On the captain's left, there is the nose landing gear steering wheel which is used at ground speeds below 70 mph to avoid losing tyres. On the co-pilot's side, there is an altitude direction (ADI) comparator used to cross-check the two ADIs. On both sides, there are banks of contact breakers normally used by ground crews when working on electrical equipment in various parts of the aircraft. Finally each flight crew member has controls for lighting and personal oxygen supply.

At this point, an example of how the flight crew members co-relate in practice should be given. The dropping of paratroops involves each member as follows. First the operation depends on the captain who must precisely position the aircraft. Beside him, the co-pilot is map-reading and advising on the final vital approach. Then there is the navigator who got them to where they are and who usually works the jump lights. As for the flight engineer, he is concerned with pressurisation and other relevant systems. Finally the loadmaster down aft is seeing to the swift despatch of the troops. All in all, it is very much a team effort.

Returning to the cabin controls, prominent on the console platform between the two pilots are the four engine throttle levers and four what are called condition levers. The throttles actually control the pitch of the propeller blades. Because the powerplants are constant-speed, if more fuel is fed to the engines the airscrew blades, pitch will increase in pitch angle to absorb the extra power produced. The coarser blade makes the aircraft travel faster. Less fuel being fed to the engines gives a finer pitch and, thus, slower flight. The condition levers, are in reality big fuel cocks by means of which the engines can be stopped. They also provide a way of feathering the propellers. The throttles may be operated individually, but are almost always moved together. In addition to having fore and aft movement, the throttles incorporate a step-type mechanism at the flight idle position. When the throttle levers are stepped down and pushed forward, they progressively increase engine power – as outlined above – for, say, take-off and climb. When the throttles are lifted up the step and pulled back, they reduce thrust from the propeller through low to zero, then to reverse thrust.

Grouped round the control console, between the captain and co-pilot, are the aircraft flap control, parking brake lever, ramp and door actuator together with the autopilot panel and the instrument landing system (ILS). The latter can be used down to a minimum of 200 ft on approach, either flying manually or with the autopilot engaged (Auto ILS). Normally, 1000 ft is the minimum height for autopilot operation, other than Auto ILS.

Looking up at the roof panel, this has – from the front – engine starter buttons, oil cooler controls and fire emergency equipment including warning lights and shut-down handles. The next section of the panel rearwards is occupied by indicators and control switches for the aircraft/engine fuel system. There is a gauge showing the total amount of fuel aboard the aircraft as well as individual gauges giving the current content of each tank. This panel is laid out diagrammatically to make the control of fuel as simple as possible. There is provision for fuel transfer, also a fuel dumping facility.

69

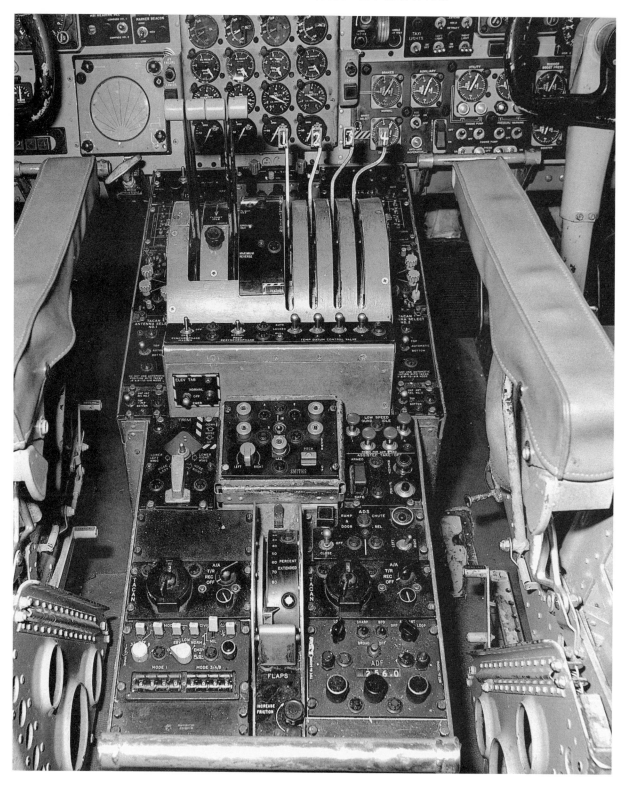

Aft of the fuel control is the electrical panel colour-coded yellow for AC and green for DC. This is followed by anti-icing gauges, which monitor the leading edges of the mainplane and tailplane, engine intakes and propeller blades, and with the applicable bleed air controls. While on the subject of colour-coding, it must be mentioned that all the aircraft emergency controls are vividly identified by black and yellow stripes like nature's warning signs for wasps, snakes and tigers. It should also be said that emergency drills, to cover every conceivable contingency, play an important part in flight training including simulator sessions.

Opposite: The central console between captain and co-pilot with the four engine throttles and four condition levers top centre.

Moving now to the navigator, he has his own set of panels immediately aft of the co-pilot. His corner contains the sophisticated instrumentation to help him with the tasks of course plotting and position checking. Among his instruments, he is provided with radar, two master compasses, automatic direction finding, read-outs for latitude and longitude, plus three other radio aids as follows:

LORAN. Long range position fixing by comparing the time differences of pulse-type transmissions from two or more radio stations.

DOPPLER. Detection of motion relative to a reflective surface by measuring the frequency shift of the radio energy.

OMEGA. Beacon based system working on very low radio frequencies over long ranges as used increasingly by aircraft.

This concludes an overall though very much abbreviated account of the Lockheed C-130

The overhead roof panel, mostly controlled by the flight engineer. The four engine starter buttons are bottom (ie, front) left.

Hercules as stationed at and operated by RAF Lyneham. From the foregoing it should be evident that the aircraft is a surprisingly versatile one. In the chapters which follow, text and pictures will show how the Lyneham Hercules fleet is kept serviceable, supported and flown over the many types of missions. Just as the air crew has to exhibit close-knit team work to fly their aircraft efficiently, so not one but a whole series of ground teams – with a further back-up of even more teams – are necessary to keep each Hercules in the air. Success is achieved by a combination of sheer professionalism and sustained enthusiasm.

Finished in a high-gloss paint scheme, XV190 was the first Hercules delivered to RAF Lyneham. Here it is seen outside the Terminal Building on delivery day, 1 August 1967. (Photo by Adrian Balch)

In dramatic contrast to the preceding picture is this photograph of XV298 celebrating One Million Hours of C130 operations.

Main picture: Hercules CMk1 XV185 in its natural element.
(Photo by Huw Roberts)

Crossing the M4 motorway close to Lyneham, the aircraft shows well the planform of the Hercules CMk1.

Hercules in formation over the Wiltshire countryside. (Photo by Adrian Balch)

ROYAL AIR FORCE

185

Another shot of XV185 seen over RAF Lyneham on 27 July 1988 when captained by Flt Lt Ade Dickson.

An airdrop from the open rear ramp of a C130.

Right: Paratroops deploying in a string.

Opposite top: Two F4 Phantoms accompany a tanker Hercules 'somewhere over the Falkland Islands'.

Opposite bottom: A CMk1 Hercules, this time acting as receiver aircraft from a Handley Page Victor tanker aircraft. (Photo by Huw Roberts)

Above & opposite inset:
Two views of in-flight
refuelling seen from
donor and receiver
aircraft. (Photos by
Adrian Balch)

Hercules-to-Hercules
refuelling.

Main picture: The unique Hercules W.Mk2, XV208, is operated by the Meteorological Research Flight from Farnborough. Nicknamed 'Snoopy', it is a regular visitor to RAF Lyneham for servicing. (Photo by Adrian Balch)

There is little in the way of maintenance work that cannot be undertaken in Lyneham's Engineering Wing hangars. Here a C130 is undergoing a major overhaul.

Right: The motive power for the Hercules comes from four Allison T56 jet turbo-props. This cutaway illustration shows the turbines and combustion chambers, and the remote reduction gearbox, upon the front shaft of which is mounted the propeller. (Courtesy Allison Gas Turbine)

A mobile crane being
used to install an
overhauled powerplant.

Operational requirements mean that, large aircraft though it is, the Hercules must be flown at low level. This is a training sortie amongst the Welsh Valleys. (Photo by Dave Fry)

Inset: Much flight training, for navigators and flight engineers as well as pilots, can be carried out in the highly realistic simulators which can operate round the clock, in all weathers and at a fraction of the hourly operating cost of the actual aircraft.

Four photographs which
show the pilots' positions
and the instrument panels
and central control console.

Above: By convention the Captain of an aircraft always sits in the left-hand seat. Note the Pilot's flight plan clipped to the control wheel and the calculator/stopwatch strapped to his leg.

Above right: The Hercules hold can be configured in a multitude of ways best suited to the load being carried. Here is a typical arrangement showing the lightweight seating.

Below: The Navigator's station, which is dominated by three vertical stacks of navigational and communications equipment, a panel of flight instruments and a radar scope.

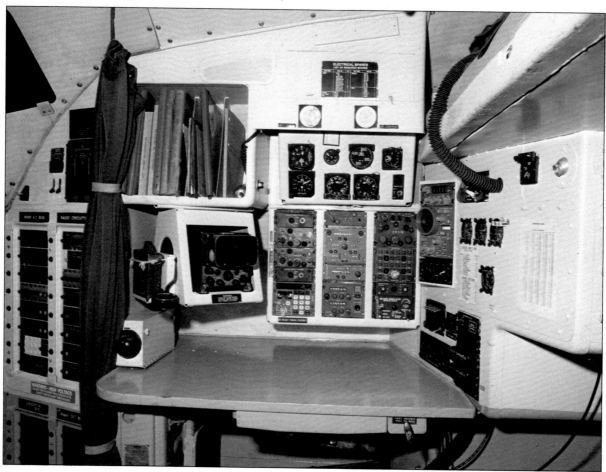

A good example of the type of service vehicle loads that the Hercules is routinely asked to carry, although even the cavernous C130 couldn't manage this lot in one bite!

The Lyneham Motor Transport pool includes everything from Minis to Snowblowers.

Main picture: **Here a C130 shows off its ultra-short, rough-ground landing capability. This capacity is more than just a party-piece, it is a vital ability in war and also when providing relief support.**

Much needed supplies being unloaded during a famine relief operation in Ethiopia.

The Operations Room at Lyneham. The large board in the background shows the state of each current flight and carries a map of the air station with the runways marked prominently.

RAF Lyneham's gate guardian, the de Havilland Comet Mk 2c once operated by 216 Squadron. (Photo by Adrian Balch)

Chapter 5
RESIDENT SQUADRONS

The four resident operational squadrons at RAF Lyneham – Nos 24, 30, 47 and 70, all take part in the non-stop route flying tasks of tactical air transport. Additionally Nos 24 and 30 squadrons carry out tanking and flight refuelling operations while Nos 47 and 70 specialise in air dropping of personnel and supplies. Each Lyneham squadron can 'field' over 20 air crews consisting of captain, co-pilot, navigator, flight engineer and air loadmaster. Thus, together with the flying instructors of No.242 Operational Conversion Unit, which further trains and improves resident squadron flying skills, Lyneham has up to 100 crews for its 60 Hercules Aircraft. This is not a surplus but a necessity when meeting emergencies in addition to heavy routine responsibilities.

The old idea of close-knit crews with their own aircraft no longer applies. To begin with, all the Hercules are available to all crews according to the type of task and depending on serviceability. Similarly, crew members are hand-picked for various missions. This arrangement makes for close-knit squadrons. As one squadron commander put it, the system 'works very well in practice'. Each crew member on each task gives of his best through a blend of comradeship and professionalism.

Before introducing the separate squadrons and outlining their interesting histories, there are many factors common to all four of them. Their headquarter buildings, which look small and quiet outside, are surprisingly extensive and active inside. The front entrance or hall contains displays of memorabilia, paintings and photographs of successful actions, lists of locations, commanders, battle honours. In each case there is an operations room with a nearby crew room, also executive offices for the squadron and flight commanders, adjutant and administrators. The senior officer of each air crew category – captain, co-pilot, navigator, etc – is responsible for that section.

Prominent on the walls of operations rooms and executive offices are large perspex panels divided into grids and covered by coloured hand-markings. In the operations room, for example, the headings list tasks, routes, crews, estimated times of departure (ETD) and estimated times of arrival (ETA). Panels cover monthly programmes with the remainder of last month's tasks nearing completion, next month's new tasks looming ahead and future tasks to be planned. More panels in the flight commanders' offices detail input responsibilities. The method might seem antiquated in this age of computerised information technology, but it is clearly visible and instantly amendable. Moreover, it confers responsibility on the writer as well as the reader.

Lyneham squadron crews work an average 24-25 days a month planning, preparing, flying and training. Apart from specific air operations, the station maintains a system of one duty working crew, two 6-hour (notice) crews and four 24-hour crews. These are provided in rotation by the squadrons when working normally. All keep in touch with their headquarters which as one nameless crew member murmured, 'can be a bit wearing socially'. By way of compensation, crew rooms are made as comfortable as possible with a food and beverage bar included. No alcohol is available except at official parties and even then availability is tempered by considerations of maintaining personal efficiency.

Reading through Lyneham squadron schedules reveals the high proportion of time spent on training. The very walls carry reminders to all concerned regarding local circuits, instrument flying, ground school (every 6 weeks), sessions on the simulators (every 2 months), dinghy drill (every 6 months), low level capability (every year when the crew is 'off-squadron' for a fortnight). Then there are various aspects of training flights, route flying in the UK, special skills in air-to-air refuelling, air dropping and formation flying, plus all the other checks to keep air personnel at the peak of efficiency. Life on a squadron is no sinecure. As another nameless crew member put it 'to fly with the rest of the squadron, you have to prove that you are safe'.

Each squadron has its own badge and there is an overall one for the station. Starting with the station badge, this shows a star-spanned world under which Lyneham's multifarious activities are summed up with Caesar-like simplicity – 'Support, save, supply'. In the cases of the squadrons, old origins, locations, exploits and often classically-minded commanders have provided some intriguing badges. The badge of No.24 Squadron is a game bird and

The badges of Nos 24, 30, 47, and 70 Squadrons.

the Latin motto 'In omnia parati' which translates as 'In all things prepared' or 'Ready for anything'. No.30 Squadron sports a palm tree denoting its sojourn in the Middle East and a French motto 'Ventre a terre'. This is an old racing term meaning 'belly to ground' which stems from the fact that the faster a horse runs the closer its body moves towards the earth. It is best translated as 'flat out' and is linked to early low-level roles of the squadron. For No.47 Squadron, another bird is depicted: a demoiselle crane which migrates from South Russia to the Sudan. No 47's motto reads, 'Nili nomen roboris omen' meaning 'The name of the Nile is the source of our strength'. As for No.70 Squadron, its badge shows a winged lion which mythical beast once stood for the might of Assyria. No.70 points out that the winged lion represents both their many years in Iraq between the wars and flying with Napier Lion engines. The squadron motto however is more to the present day point. It is the single Latin word 'Usquam' which translates simply as 'Anywhere'.

No.24 Squadron is the senior squadron at Lyneham and the sixth most senior in the Royal Air Force. It was formed at Hounslow on the 1st September 1915 and moved to France in February 1916 to become the first squadron operating DH2 single-seat fighters. The squadron's first commanding officer was Major L.G. Hawker VC, DSO who was later shot down and killed by Baron Von Richthofen. By the end of World War I, No.24 Squadron had accounted for no less than 297 enemy aircraft.

During the interwar years, No.24 was engaged in communication duties, a role which it continued and developed during World War II. As one of the leading squadrons in Transport Command, it was privileged, not only to carry His Majesty King George VI, but also to operate Sir Winston Churchill's personal Avro York. In recognition of its 323 flights with unarmed Lockheed Hudsons into besieged Malta, No.24 Squadron was accorded the singular honour of delivering the island's George Cross Medal.

In 1947 the squadron was reorganised on a Commonwealth basis and until 1962 many of its commanding officers and members were drawn from the air forces of Australia, Canada and New Zealand. During 1948-49, the squadron's Dakotas played a prominent part in the Berlin Airlift. Throughout the post-war years, No.24 transported numerous VIP's including Field Marshal Montgomery, Marshal of the RAF Lord Tedder and many foreign dignitaries. A change of role gradually took place after 1950 with the acquisition of Handley Page Hastings. An increased number of schedule flights were carried out whilst the VIP requirements decreased.

In March 1954, No.24 Squadron received the Queen's Standard, the first transport squadron to gain such an honour. The Standard carried the maximum permissible number of battle honours – Western Front 1914-18, the Somme 1916, Hindenburg Line and Low Countries 1939-40, Malta 1942, North Africa 1942-43 and Burma 1944-45.

No.24 Squadron moved to Lyneham in January 1968 where it was re-equipped with the Lockheed C-130 Hercules. Operations using this aircraft have included famine relief in Nepal 1973, the evacuation of refugees from Cyprus in 1974, the airlift of medical supplies to the earthquake victims of Turkey in 1976, the transport of Red Cross supplies to Phnom Penh in 1979, the evacuation of refugees from Iran also in 1979, the airlift of the peace keeping force into Rhodesia in 1980, the massive airlift of supplies for the South Atlantic Task Force in 1982 and delivery of relief supplies in famine-stricken Ethiopia during 1985.

Stuart Castle was No.24 Squadron's first pilot, who went out to fight over the Western Front and survived.
In 1971 Mr Castle returned to fly again with 24 Squadron. He also tried the simulator and made 'a very fine circuit'.

The squadron played a prominent part in the Berlin Airlift and was presented with a Gold Cup by the grateful citizens.

Following their part in the Falklands campaign, six of Lyneham's Hercules fleet were converted for air-to-air refuelling duties as tanker aircraft. This involved installing four tanks in the hold, each tank containing 7000 lb of fuel. No.24 Squadron crews were in the forefront of this development and continued air bridge work until early in 1989. During that period, crews were rotated every four months while aircraft were converted as and when major servicing became due.

Currently the squadron has three roles. Its main role is that of Strategic Air Transport (SAT) carrying service personnel and supplies worldwide. Its specialist role is the Air-to-Air Refuelling (AAR) described above and there is also a limited Air Landing role performed from time to time. Thus life at No.24 very much depends on the versatility of both the Hercules aircraft and its crews. 'Ready for anything', indeed.

No.24 Squadron has links with the Birmingham University Squadron and No.93 City of Bath Air Training Corps Squadron. These links help to promote interest in flying and attract newcomers to the Royal Air Force. Another noteworthy link maintained by No.24 is adoption by the squadron of the Burton Hill House School for physically-handicapped children in Malmesbury. Support for this most worthy cause includes fund-raising and organising social events for the children, events which are enjoyed by the squadron members and, of course, the children themselves.

There is much friendly rivalry between the Lyneham squadrons and, on the subject of formation, No.30 will readily point out that it began at Farnborough in November 1914. However the unit was untitled when it sailed for Egypt and not designated No.30 Squadron until the 24th March 1915. During World War I No.30 was engaged on a wide range of duties including fighter, bomber, reconnaissance and army co-operation throughout the Middle East. So, as well as plenty of action, it saw a great many palm trees like the one in the squadron badge.

During this period, No.30 Squadron gained the distinction of carrying out the first air transport support operations when its modified BE2C, Farman and Short aircraft dropped supplies to beleaguered British Forces. Supplies dropped included flour, sugar, salt, medical stores, wireless parts, engine components and even a millstone attached to a parachute. The corn was dropped by placing the full sack in a large sack which received the corn when the small sack burst on impact. It was the shape of things to come for in the Ethiopian famine relief operation 70 years later, Lyneham Hercules crew used triple-sacking for such air drops.

Between the wars, No.30 Squadron operated in what was then Persia, Iraq and Kurdistan using DH9A, Westland Wapiti and Hawker Hardy aircraft. The DH9A's, with cruising speeds around 75 mph, were exchanged for Wapitis in 1929 and Hardys in 1935. Most operations

Presentation of Standard to No.24 Squadron on 15th September 1981 by the Princess Royal, Honorary Air Commodore, RAF Lyneham.

During and after World War 1, No.30 Squadron was active throughout the Middle East, seen here with a DH9A in Iraq in 1929.

Between the wars, 30
Squadron flew DH9As,
Westland Wapitis (shown
here) and Hawker Hardys
in Iraq, Persia and
Kurdistan.

'The Real Thing'.
Blenheims of 30
Squadron going into
action over Greece in
November 1940.

in those days consisted of trying to maintain peace among warring tribes. During 1938, command of No.30 Squadron was held by Sqn Ldr G.H. Stainforth AFC, previously a member of the RAF's Special High Speed Flight, who in 1931 established a world speed record of 407.5 mph in a Supermarine S6B.

Throughout World War II, the squadron saw action in Egypt, Greece, Ceylon, India and Burma, flying Blenheims, Hurricanes and Thunderbolts. This history of No.30 is full of adventures and misadventures. One pilot had to force land his Hurricane on a carrier – with no arrester hook – and did this so successfully the Navy declared him an honorary instructor. Another had to force land, after an air battle, on a marine promenade. In December 1946, the

No.30 Squadron added Hurricanes to their Blenheims for yet more action in North Africa and later Burma.

Beverley transport aircraft operated by 30 Squadron during the 1950/60s in the Middle East and Indian Ocean areas.

squadron was reduced to a 'number only' status after 31 years spent overseas.

No.30 reformed in November 1947 with Dakota aircraft. After service in support of the Berlin Airlift, the squadron was re-equipped with Valettas in January 1951. In April 1957, No.30 was re-equipped once more, this time with Blackburn Beverleys and in November 1959 again moved abroad. Operating from Eastleigh in Kenya until 1964, the squadron flew a variety of missions including taking supplies to typhoon-ravaged Mauritius, and food to famine-stricken villages in Africa and evacuating refugees from the Congo.

From Kenya, No.30 Squadron moved to Bahrain where it remained until its second reduction to 'number only' status in September 1967. Reforming once more in June 1968 at Fairford with Hercules aircraft, the squadron operated from there until moving to Lyneham in 1971. Since reforming, crews of No.30 Squadron have visited most parts of the world on routine and special missions. As with the other Hercules squadrons at Lyneham, it took part in such operations as the Dacca disaster airlift, the Philippines and Nicaragua flood relief operations, the reinforcement of Belize, the deployment and recovery of UK monitoring forces to Rhodesia (prior to that country's independence as Zimbabwe) and the famine relief mission in Ethiopia.

No.30 Squadron played a prominent part in the Falklands War. From the onset the squadron was flying vital supplies to Ascension Island even before the Task Force ships had left England. At the same time Lyneham started fitting Hercules with probes for air-to-air refuelling. These were used to receive from the Victor tankers at Ascension and maintained the incredible air bridge which carried passengers and freight over the 4000 miles to Stanley. The flying by Lyneham crews during that operation commanded the respect of other air forces and admiration of the civilian world. By 1990, No.30 will have completed 75 years service, 41 overseas. 'Perhaps not Lyneham's senior squadron', someone remarked, 'but undeniably the oldest'.

We turn now to No.47 Squadron, which was formed on the 1st March 1916 at Beverley in the East Riding of Yorkshire and in September of that year went to Salonika in Greece. There, under very primitive conditions, it mounted more than 5,500 sorties throughout World War I. Then in April 1919, the squadron was sent to South Russia to help White Russian forces in their ill-fated resistance.

Between the two world wars – operating Bristol Fighters, Fairey IIIFs, Vickers Vincents and Wellesleys – No.47 Squadron was based in East Africa notably at Khartoum in the Sudan. It is from this period that the squadron badge (the crane which migrates from South Russia

A photograph of a No.47 Squadron Fairey Gordon flying over the desert near Khartoum. Note squadron number on the front fuselage.

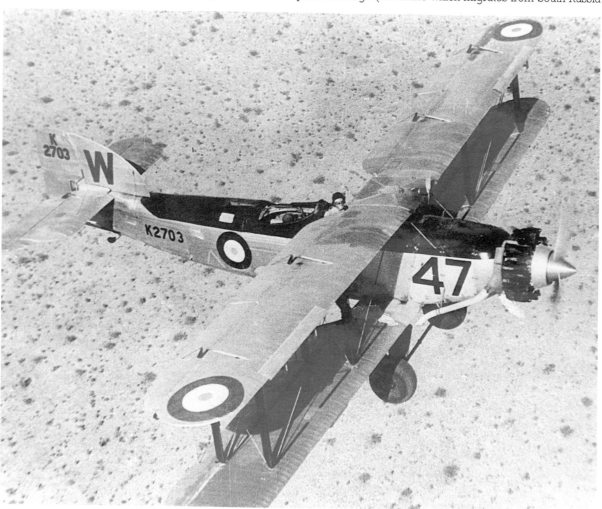

to the Sudan) and the motto referring to the Nile (the Blue and White Niles combine at Khartoum) were conceived. There the squadron performed a variety of roles mainly connected with maintaining peace between warring tribes.

In 1940, the squadron's eight Wellesleys attacked the Italian-occupied airfield at Asmara in Eritrea inflicting considerable damage on the hangars and runways. For the next 18 months, using all aircraft and resources available, No.47 Squadron continued to harass the enemy. When the Italian forces in Abyssinia surrendered during May 1941, the squadron moved south to Asmara and continued operations until the East African campaign was successfully concluded in November.

In January 1942, the squadron redeployed in Northern Egypt for an entirely new maritime role. For almost two years it either attacked enemy shipping or protected Allied convoys in the Mediterranean. For these operations, No.47 was equipped first with Beauforts and later with Beaufighters. The squadron extended its activities from the Nile delta and Palestine coast area to as far afield as Sardinia, Corsica and the shores of Italy. Later, in 1943, No.47 squadron aircraft were pitted against German Bf 109s over the Agean and suffered heavy losses. For one task alone the squadron lost three aircraft yet gained a DSO, a DFC and three DFMs.

For No.47 Squadron it seemed a never-ending war. No sooner had German activity declined in the Mediterranean than the squadron was re-equipped with Mosquitoes and sent east during 1944 to combat the Japanese in Burma and Malaya. Taking the month of March 1945 alone, No.47 mounted more than 230 sorties, totalling 964 flying hours in support of the Army's assault on Mandalay. After further operations in South East Asia, No.47 Squadron was disbanded on the 21st March 1946.

On the 1st September 1946, No.47 – which had been disbanded in the Far East – was reformed in the Middle East and returned almost at once to Fairford, England where it operated Halifax transports. In 1948 it became the first squadron to operate the Hastings, and later that year took part in the Berlin Airlift. In 1956 the squadron was

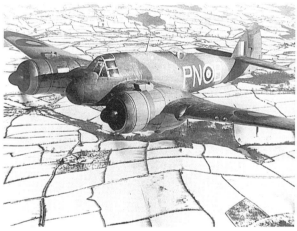

After collecting their Beaufighters from wartime snow-covered England, 47 Squadron took them to fight in North Africa and in the Middle East.

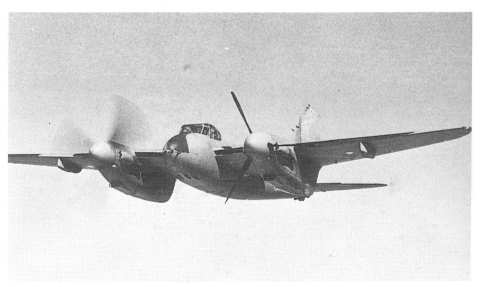

A de Havilland Mosquito with one propeller feathered and damage to the tail fin. No.47 Squadron used these amazing wooden aircraft against the Japanese.

re-equipped with Beverleys and continued to operate these aircraft until 1968. No.47 Squadron then returned to Fairford for conversion to the Hercules and finally moved to Lyneham in 1971. In December 1971 the squadron made two much publicised flights into East Pakistan to evacuate civilian personnel caught up in the war between East and West Pakistan. For his and the squadron's part in the evacuation, Wg Cdr Hannah, the Squadron Commander, was awarded the Air Force Cross.

Flying coalmen. During the Berlin Airlift, 47 Squadron's share of lifting coal and everything else liftable was 22,000 tons in 3000 flights.

In 1982 the squadron was heavily involved in the Falklands Campaign during which it was tasked with resupply work at Ascension Island. Flights of up to 24 hours were commonplace and, for their efforts, the squadron was awarded South Atlantic Battle Honours. Before and since then, the duties and deployments of No.47 continue worldwide. Squadron crews are continually visiting European countries, Canada and the United States, Middle East and Far East, coping with disasters and famine relief. In addition No.47 Squadron has accompanied members of the Royal Family on tours round the world, competed in NATO competitions and supported the RAF Red Arrows team. The wide interests of this ever-active squadron range from taking part in a James Bond film to maintaining close links with local community projects such as adopting the Middlefield School for Mentally Handicapped Children at nearby Chippenham.

Operation Bushel was the code name for the RAF's famine relief efforts in Ethiopia. Two Lyneham Hercules flown by No.47 in background.

No.47 Squadron
'exercising' a Hercules
over the Nevada Desert.
Some Americans said
the RAF seemed to be
operating a different
type of Hercules.

No.70 Squadron (or LXX as it historically prefers to call itself) began like the other three operational squadrons at Lyneham during the grim days of World War I. It was formed at Farnborough on the 22nd April 1916 with Sopwith 1-1/2 Strutters – the first RFC aircraft with a gun firing through the propeller arc and an observer sitting behind the pilot – and crossed to France during the middle of 1916. No.70 arrived during the struggle for aerial supremacy concurrent with the Battle of the Somme. Next, during the early months of 1917, it was caught up in the battles of Arras and Messine – or rather above them – duelling with enemy formations under the formidable Baron Von Richthofen. The squadron is proud to record that one of its early commanding officers was a Major A.W. Tedder, later to become Marshal of the Royal Air Force, Lord Tedder.

France 1916. No.70 Squadron shown with their Sopwith 1½-Strutters, the first RFC aircraft with a gun firing through the propeller arc.

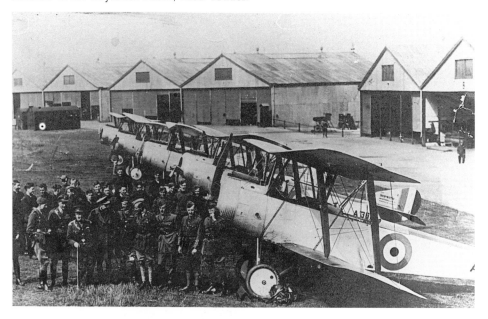

During the 1920s, 70 Squadron in Iraq first operated Vickers Vernons with Napier Lion engines – hence the Assyrian Lion squadron badge.

In July 1917, No.70 Squadron was re-equipped with Sopwith Camels and operated these until disbandment in 1920. A year later, No.58 Squadron based in Egypt with Handley Page 0/400s and Vickers Vikings was renumbered LXX. The following year the squadron moved to Iraq where it remained until 1938.

The outbreak of World War II found No.70 squadron once more in Egypt, this time with Vickers Valentias to be replaced a year later by Wellingtons. During the war, the squadron's bases depended on the fluctuating fortunes of the Allied Armies in North Africa. No.70 was there as each battle was fought then, in December 1943, moved with the armies to Italy where it remained until the end of the war. The evocative names of World War II are included in this very active squadron's story: Benghasi, Tobruk, Alamein, Crete, Palermo, Turin, Brenner Pass, moving steadily on to Greece and the Balkans, Austria and the German heartland.

After flying their Wellingtons right through the war, No.70 squadron was re-equipped with Liberators in January 1945. Their last bombing mission was an attack on German marshalling yards at Freilassing. Then came the outbreak of peace and No.70 was moved back to Egypt for disbandment. Two weeks later it reappeared when No.178 Squadron, equipped with Lancasters, became LXX. The same exercise occurred a year later. The squadron was disbanded and No.125 Squadron, equipped with Dakotas, was renumbered LXX. Dark mutterings likened No.70, not to the mythical Assyrian lion, but to the Phoenix forever rising from its own ashes.

In the late 1930s, the squadron was re-equipped with Vickers Valentias powered by Bristol Pegasus engines.

World War II found 70 Squadron operating Wellington bombers in the Western Desert then on to Italy.

The 1950s saw the squadron serving in the Suez Canal zone. In 1955, No.70 moved to Cyprus where it received Hastings transports. In 1967 the Hastings were replaced by Argosys which were subsequently supplanted by Hercules. The squadron moved from Akrotiri to Lyneham in 1975 thereby completing 55 years around the Middle East.

The 1980s opened with No.70 Squadron crews helping in the Rhodesian Cease Fire Mission and with a relief operation in Nepal. The latter was described as 'particularly interesting' as some of the dropping zones (DZs) were 8000 ft above sea level and surrounded by even higher mountains. Then came the Falklands conflict to which No.70 was fully committed maintaining the long range supply routes across the South Atlantic. On one such trip, with air-to-air refuelling, a No.70 Squadron crew was airborne for over 28 hours. Later in May 1984, the squadron received South Atlantic Battle Honours. This resulted in a new squadron standard presented by Her Royal Highness, The Princess Anne and the old standard was laid up in Lyneham Parish Church.

During 1984 famine struck North Africa particularly Ethiopia which was also blighted by civil war. Commencing on the 1st November that year, No.70 Squadron led the biggest famine relief operation ever conducted by the RAF. Six Lyneham Hercules, staged through Cyprus, arrived at Addis Ababa on the 3rd and 4th of November. There, in a tented town around the airport, the 80-strong Lyneham detachment was to live and operate for the next fourteen months. No.70's efforts in Ethiopia, combined with those of other Lyneham units, were in the best traditions of its long history. In 1986, No.70 completed its seventy years as Seventy Squadron.

The foregoing are but potted histories of the four operational squadrons based at RAF Lyneham. Each squadron zealously records its full history with photographs and other memorabilia assembled for new members to follow. Today, in an age when self-interest is all too rife, it is a tonic to talk to squadron crews where the reverse pertains. If only, one reflects, this spirit could be applied nationally. Members are modest about their

In November 1984, 70 Squadron led the biggest famine relief operation (Bushel) in Ethiopia ever conducted by the RAF.

achievements, more pleased to relate how they helped in particular situations ranging from the difficult to the near impossible at the time.

At the time of the Falklands, for example, the idea of an air bridge across the wastes of the South Atlantic seemed impossible. Although it could be done technically, to maintain it was quite another matter. In other words the machines and methods were at hand but it needed people of sufficient skill and determination to succeed. Talking to crew members who made these prodigious efforts, also following their routes on charts, brings home to one what was involved. The following figures, based on average cruising speeds, outline the problems faced.

Lyneham-Dakar 2550 miles $8\frac{1}{2}$ hours flying

Dakar-Ascension 1350 miles $4\frac{1}{2}$ hours flying

Ascension-Falklands 3900 miles 13 hours flying

The last stage seemed to be the clincher. It should not be forgotten that, with the Falklands occupied by the then enemy and the Task Force still at sea, a heavily laden aircraft leaving Ascension was – as it were – launching itself into a void. The trick could only be done if other aircraft refuelled it and this was achieved, day and night, under some of the world's worst weather conditions.

That was not all. When receiving fuel from Victor or VC10 tanker aircraft, Lyneham Hercules had to 'toboggan'. This further trick was evolved because the jet-powered tanker aircraft's stalling speed was close to the maximum speed of the turboprop-powered Hercules. How did the latter attain a refuelling speed compatible with that of the jets? It did this by a long, shallow, carefully controlled descent from 20,000 ft down to 10,000 ft – the jet using air brakes, the Hercules flat out. And still that was not all. Another consideration was a time slot of less than twenty minutes to make contact and refuel or fail. Flying two dissimilar aircraft at such limits – they have to be within 80ft of each other when air-to-air refuelling contact is made, reducing to 40ft – requires considerable skill. Neither at the time of the Falklands nor since have sufficient people realised the concentrated effort of the RAF crew members concerned necessary to carry out such manoeuvres. At least the subsequent conversion of some Hercules to tanker aircraft has eliminated 'tobogganing'. Now Hercules refuel Hercules at the same speeds and altitudes with difficulties minimised through training and repetition.

Lyneham air crews talk more readily about missions of mercy and they are especially pleased about the parts they played in the Ethiopian famine relief operation. There, Hercules based at Addis Ababa would fly to Port Assab on the Red Sea coast to pick up their loads. The grain would then be airlifted to inland strips. Each evening, after a hard day's loading and flying the aircraft, their crew would return to Addis Ababa for a hard night of servicing and repairs.

The landing strips were not so much small as high, hot and rough. Loads usually of around 30,000 lb, and often over 40,000 lb, made for tricky touchdowns at 8000 ft with temperatures in excess of 25°C. Thus these airland operations were not without their hazards. One of the first Hercules to land blew a main wheel tyre which not only reduced the numbers of tyres from four to three, but also damaged some services in the landing gear bay. The wheel was removed with some difficulty and the aircraft took off and returned to base on three main tyres. During the next five days, the detachment went through nine tyres. After that a combination of new reinforced tyres, refined landing techniques and removing the larger rocks from the strips reduced these problems.

During their 'days off' in Ethiopia, Lyneham crews did what else they could to help beat that grim emergency. For example, the RAF Medical Officer – ostensibly there to look after Air Force personnel – assisted in the treatment of famine victims. These conditions, more than those in the Falklands War, seemed to have made the deeper impression on those concerned. 'Until then,' one participant said, 'we did not realise how fortunate we were by comparison. We had to help'.

103

Early in 1985, it became evident that other Ethiopian famine areas existed in the mountains and airdrops were planned as a result. From January onwards sacks of grain were air transported and dropped. Triple bagging was used to reduce bursting. A typical drop load comprised sixteen bundles of up to twenty bags tied to wooden baseboards. These were heaved from the rear ramps at heights of 35 feet. Floor angle was critical and a high nose attitude helped, though, it was not so easy to attain so near the ground. The load cords were designed to break leaving the sacks to tumble. Over 95 per cent of the triple-bagged sacks remained intact. As for those that burst, the thousands of starving people were said to have recovered every last grain.

For the remainder of the RAF's stay in Ethiopia, two or three airdrops, each of around 16 tons, were made daily. Lyneham sent out a resupply Hercules each week for the fourteen months to rotate aircraft usage and crew changeover. When in December 1985 the last Lyneham Hercules left Addis Ababa, a grand total of 2,152 famine relief sorties had been flown and 32,158 tons delivered of which 17,778 tons were airlanded and 14,380 tons airdropped. When someone present was asked to sum up the operation, he came out with a telling remark, 'We learned so much'.

Learning – or as the RAF calls it, training – is the key to the succession of successes and the subject of the next chapter.

Chapter 6
OPERATIONAL TRAINING

RAF aircrews enjoy the highest of reputations among the world's airforces and airlines. They gained esteem during the earliest days of the service and have retained it ever since. One might well ask how this was done. The short explanation is that the RAF has always placed great emphasis on training – initial training, advanced training, refresher training, specialist training, total retraining. In fact aircrews have to think training as well as flying. Every RAF unit is subject to training disciplines and the following describes what it takes to fly Hercules at Lyneham.

The fifth flying organization at Lyneham is No.242 Operational Conversion Unit (OCU). No.242 OCU itself contains five squadrons and an ancillary flight, all of whose activities are closely interwoven with the main squadrons as follows:

Ground Training Squadron (GTS)
Hercules Conversion Squadron (HCS)
Hercules Training Squadron (HTS)
Simulator Squadron
Support Training Squadron (STS), incorporating Tanker
Training Flight (TTF)

The first four of these training squadrons are located in the station's central complex, while the specialist Support Training Squadron and Tanker Training Flight are at 'C' south site. Before describing what each does and how their collective activities are dovetailed with those of the flying squadrons, it is necessary to learn a little about No.242's previous history.

No.242 OCU was formed at RAF Dishforth in 1951 by the amalgamation of No.240 OCU from North Luffenham operating Dakotas, and No.241 at Dishforth with Hastings. While based at Dishforth the OCU also trained Valetta and Beverley aircrews. In 1962 No.242 OCU moved to RAF Thorney Island taking its Hastings and Beverley aircraft, which were joined the following year by the Argosy fleet from RAF Benson. No.242 OCU continued training courses until 1975 and the impending closure of Thorney Island. At that stage the Ground Training Squadron and Conversion Squadron of No.242 moved to RAF Lyneham. There – with the Training Squadron, Simulator Squadron and Support Training Squadron already resident at Lyneham – the new No.242 OCU was formed in November 1975.

The title Operational Conversion Unit signifies a prime objective which, in the case of Lyneham, is to convert aircrew onto Hercules aircraft. No.242 OCU meets this objective, but it is also responsible for a much wider sphere of activities. These include essential post-graduate training both on the ground and in the air, rigorous checks on standardisation and progressive improvement of abilities through personnel categorisation. In order to take one through the system the training squadrons will be treated separately though all are interconnected.

Ground Training Squadron (GTS)

This squadron covers the full span of technical, operational and professional subjects relevant to Lyneham's Hercules aircraft. Its instructors deal with four or five courses a year, each of six crews, ie 30 people. The course is very much based on the *ab initio* student and tailored to this level. It should be mentioned, however, that an ex-Hercules pilot, returning to the aircraft after other duties, starts from the beginning with the tyros. Each course last seven weeks and, though mainly classroom, includes detachments to RAF Mount Batten for survival training and dinghy drill, also to RAF North Luffenham for an insight into aviation medicine. A written exam has to be passed before moving to the next phase with the Hercules Conversion Squadron (HCS).

Above: Where flying Lyneham Hercules starts – in a classroom of No.242 Operational Conversion Unit.

Above right: One of the correl rooms in the Ground Training Squadron with trainees learning Hercules flight deck locations.

Aircrew trainees being shown the main features of a cutaway Allison T56 turboprop engine.

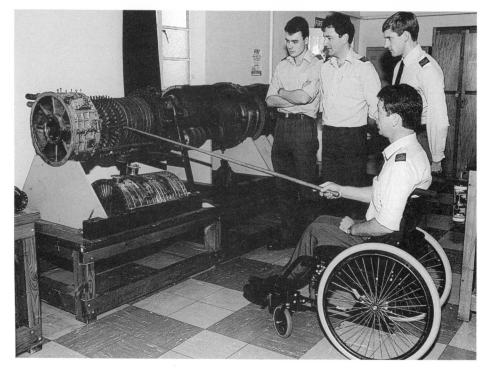

GTS occupies part of a Lyneham building adapted in 1975. Adaptations consisted of creating lecture and demonstration rooms, a process which is still continuing. There are separate lecture rooms for pilots, navigators, flight engineers and loadmasters who all learn different skills before coming together as a crew. The demonstration room contains aircraft units and equipment such as a sectioned Hercules engine, a propeller assembly and an auxiliary power unit, also workable avionic sets. Display panels showing aircraft systems are wall-mounted throughout the school. Serving the school are sections in which lecture notes, training videos and overhead projector transparencies are prepared in-house.

Upgrading of instruction material and facilities is an on-going process and currently two major improvements are underway at the Ground Training School. The first is the setting up of what are called correls (correlatives), which are simple diagrammatic displays of Hercules controls and instrumentation. Although shown diagrammatically, these are to correct size and positioning as in the aircraft control cabin. Thus aircrew trainees can sit quietly at one of the displays to learn their check lists. The word 'quietly' is important and is recognised by having each correl in a small office to aid concentration. The second training aid under construction is for the air loadmasters who at present can only learn their trade in the holds of real aircraft which are, more often than not, needed for other purposes. To close this gap in training facilities, a mock-up of the Hercules hold is being built in the school and will contain all the specialised equipment utilised by loadmasters.

Hercules Conversion Squadron (HCS)

At this squadron, trainees from the ground school are crewed-up and learn to fly the Hercules in their respective roles. The course takes eleven weeks during which captains fly 52 hours and co-pilots 76 because the latter are invariably *ab initio*. Navigators, engineers and loadmasters fly the full 76 hours since they are needed to man the aircraft regardless of whatever task is being undertaken. The syllabus includes general aircraft handling by day and night, instrument flying, navigation and route operations including international airways and Atlantic crossings.

HCS is the only squadron at Lyneham which demands a formal RAF instructor qualification for all its staff. Every pilot is a Qualified Flying Instructor (QFI) and has done the Central Flying School course then instructed at either a University Air Squadron, a Basic Flying Training School or an Advanced Flying Training School. Similarly all the navigator instructors have passed the Staff Navigation course and spent time instructing at the Air Navigation School.

Much emphasis is placed on simulator exercises which occupy at least 38 hours of trainee time. Basic procedures are covered in four 4-hour simulator sorties before actual flying, followed later by sessions in line with the syllabus. HCS instructors operate the simulator sorties as well as the flying sequences. The last phase of the course involves trainee categorisation. This is done by ground examinations, simulator tests and three distinct flying checks: basic aircraft handling, instrument rating and route operation assessment. In addition, the instructors accompany all trainees on long distance route (called 'role') flights. Wherever possible, loaded aircraft are preferred as the extra weight makes for better training, in handling by the trainee captain and co-pilot, necessary adjustments by the navigator and engineer, and actual carrying conditions for the loadmaster. Even emergencies are welcomed as these notably extend crew experience.

Two recent experiences were related. The first was when a Hercules was flying at 29,000 ft some 300 miles west of Goose Bay, Canada. Suddenly the whole aircraft began to shudder. The vibrations became worse and the problem was diagnosed in the air when one of the two starboard dinghies was seen to be wrapped round the tailplane. It was an incident which trainees would remember, as indeed would the ground crew who flew out with a new dinghy and repaired the tailplane 30ft off the ground in the bracing Canadian air.

On another HCS training flight, an aircraft was diverted from Gander to Mexico City to help in the aftermath of an earthquake. This diversion worked wonders with their navigational training as they had to travel via Belize in Central America to pick up servicemen and supplies.

Towards the end of their conversion course, trainees are asked both for their squadron posting preference and also tested to ascertain whether they would suit their chosen duties. Although there are no hard and fast rules, older crew members tend to opt for Nos 24 and 30 squadrons, which have tanker as well as route flying responsibilities, while younger members go more for the low-level tasks as carried out by Nos 47 and 70 Squadrons. Postings are finally decided by a panel of Lyneham OCU instructors and personnel staff at No.1 Group Headquarters, Upavon. Trainees leaving conversion courses for squadron duties are regarded as 'still inexperienced' and thus graded 'D' category. A strict check is kept of their ability and proficiency by the squadrons in conjunction with No.242 OCU to which they will return, again and again, for further training.

Hercules Training Squadron (HTS)

This third OCU organisation sited next to the Ground Training Squadron, is the one responsible for further training, testing and checking of aircrew standards within the Lyneham Hercules fleet. These aims are achieved by Periodic Refresher Training (PRT), intermediate assessments between PRT's and rigorous route work. With regard to Periodic Refresher Training courses, undertaken by every squadron aircrew member, it comprises two weeks of intensive training culminating in a full-scale categorisation review. All training is carefully documented and the ensuing review will either confirm or improve the category held. The PRT programme consists of five flying sorties, four simulator sessions and further ground training lessons with each element having a bearing on categorisation.

Periodic Refresher Training, as applied by No.242 OCU's Hercules Training Squadron, continues throughout the flying career of every aircrew member. Its frequency, however, depends on the overall category held by that member. 'D' Category aircrew personnel have to take the refresher course every six months, 'C' Category (regarded as average) yearly, 'B' Category (above average) every 18 months and the exceptional 'A' Category every 2 years.

These details of aircrew training and checking have been given to illustrate a process which, while intensive and unrelenting, is positive and rewarding. The system provides every facility and encouragement so that individuals can reach their highest potential, and instructors will give limitless extra time to help pupils achieve this. Furthermore it is understood by all concerned that all instructors go through the same system with even stricter criteria. When instruction staff were asked what motivated trainees – was it fear of failing – they all replied, 'On the contrary. The driving force is pride. To do better and to succeed'.

While the PRT course is a formidable one, it does have certain features, definitely beneficial to aircrew members, which must be mentioned here. Every month the Hercules Training Squadron takes a single crew from each of Lyneham's operational squadrons for the two-week course. The word single is relevant because it means that the five aircrew members involved receive one-to-one tuition; which is said to be the secret of success at Eton. This makes what might be regarded as yet another course into a privilege, all the more so because HTS staff members are Flight Instructors, and the pilots are of captaincy category. There can be no better way to improve flying skills than by benefiting from others' experience.

On the subject of staff, these instructors themselves undergo Monthly Continuation Training (MCT) involving two hours on the simulator and at least one and a half hours flying. Their continuing exercises are to assess and self-assess capabilities. They too, take on station tasks – such as routine flights to RAF Germany or helping out on other squadron's co-pilot training – both to assist, and to refine their own techniques. Extra duties occur about every six weeks and are fitted between the two-week PRT course which they superintend every month. So what with pre-course preparations, post-course assessments, their non-monthly continuation training also helping out whenever possible, HTS staff have full yearly programmes.

Like other training instructors, they stressed the added benefits to be gained from emergencies. At such times it is 'all hands to the pump' and most instructors had a favourite story to tell which added to collective knowledge. One pilot instructor was in Central Africa where he was called upon to use a large level plain as an airfield. He arrived during the dry season when the iron-hard ground was covered in long grass. His landing proved uneventful but, on commencing his take-off run, the Hercules pilot found he could not hold the aircraft in a straight line. Instead he was being led round a wide curve and wisely he abandoned his take-off to learn the reason why.

On examining the ground he discovered that the Hercules nose and main wheels were located in what looked like giant tram lines. These deep grooves, previously hidden by the grass, had been made by another aircraft taxying on the plain during the wet season when hard earth was soft mud. The pilot summed up the incident: 'One should always expect the unexpected after training for every conceivable contingency.'

Simulator Squadron

The phrase 'every conceivable contingency' logically brings this account of No.242 OCU's activities to that of its Simulator Squadron. As has been mentioned, simulator training forms an integral part of HCS and HTS courses. There are three full-mission advanced flight simulators at Lyneham – amongst the most modern in the Royal Air Force. Each cost £3½ million to which must be added software at £250,000 per visual system. From the outside, the three simulator blocks look solid and quiet. Inside all is activity from early in the morning until late at night. Collectively the three simulators and operating staff provide some 6000 hours of training time a year.

The Lyneham flight simulators are used for a variety of tasks, some of which have already been mentioned. These activities are now listed to show the overall range:

Hercules conversion courses
Periodic refresher training
Monthly aircrew sessions
Research agencies usage
Foreign air force assistance
Demonstration and maintenance

Apart from maintenance and administration staff, the simulators are manned by two specialist teams. The first is composed of simulator instructors who are all qualified Hercules pilots or air engineers. It will

A flight simulator mobile cabin at rest. Each of the three Lyneham simulators cost £3½ million.

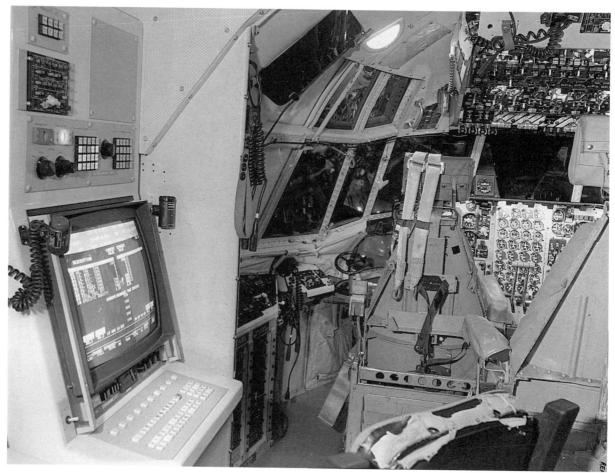

Inside, the simulator cabin is fitted out exactly like a Hercules flight deck – but with instructor's panel, left.

be appreciated that with such an important task instructors have to be of the highest calibre. No.242 OCU insists that these personnel have current or at least very recent Hercules operating experience and, in consequence, they emanate straight from flying squadrons. It is OCU policy that each instructor spends about a year on the Simulator Squadron before moving to HCS or HTS. Thus the simulators also provide a source of pilot and air engineer instructors for the two training squadrons. The second specialist team is made up of simulator console personnel, all of whom are highly qualified Air Electronics Operators (AEOPs). These, drawn from the maritime fleet, simulate air traffic control agencies, manage the visual system and generally look after safety in what is called the Motion Hall.

Each flight simulator complex is built around a Motion Hall having internal dimensions of 40 ft cubed. The simulator module within the cube consists of a box-like structure mounted on six long-stroke hydraulic jacks. Steps lead up to a door at the rear of the module. Before a simulator session, the steps are lowered thereby leaving the jacks free to manipulate the module through six axes of motion. Adjacent to each Motion hall is its console room. The three Lyneham simulators 'A', 'B' and 'C', are served by a central mainframe computer room. All rooms are air-conditioned.

Built inside the simulator module is an exact reproduction of a Hercules flight deck. All the controls, buttons, indicators, dials, radios and avionics are present with seating for the captain, co-pilot, flight engineer and navigator. In addition to crew seating, there are two positions on the port rear side for a pilot instructor and an engineer instructor. The simulator

A Hercules captain and co-pilot undergoing a regular simulator session.

visual system is projected on four screens fitted outside the captain's and co-pilots forward- and side-facing windows. Its data base covers the world so that approaches to most military and civil airfields can be reproduced.

Likewise the simulator has memory banks containing all navigational data for route flying, airfield approaches and landings. Programmes include dusk and night landings with nearby urban lights as well as those of airfield lighting. There are facilities for map reading, instrument flying and radio communications, the latter containing distortions and chatter from other aircraft to make them realistic. Similarly there are typical weather forecasts. Sessions cover the whole spectrum of normal functions and an alarmingly wide range of malfunctions. The latter are deliberately introduced to test trainees. They may take the form of an errant result on their check list or the necessity (and drill) to shut down not one but two engines. Other simulated tests include search-and-rescue missions down to such details as looking for survivor flares.

The Simulator Squadron has a forward planning room where such sessions are programmed on two wall charts – one for the current week and the other for the following week. A glance at these charts will confirm the heavy demands on simulator time and instructor attendance. A typical day is from 0730 to 2200 hours which means a 0630 start for instructors and, more often than not, post-training work until well after midnight. Records are kept on the performance of each trainee using the simulator and the tests applied are also varied every 3, 6 and 12 months. For example, during early simulator sessions an engine failure or an aborted take-off will be introduced. At least every six months the crew has to deal with a two-engined approach while the yearly tests could include 'crashing and ditching'.

The average time of a squadron aircrew session in the simulator is two hours though for initial and refresher training these are stepped up to four hours. Before each session there is a briefing just as prior to a real flight with a full range of documents, route information, call signs and meteorological reports. Defects and emergencies used in simulator programmes do not remain the same. The latest incidents received from Lockheed, which has hundreds of Hercules flying worldwide with other air forces, are regularly relayed to RAF Lyneham. These are fed into the simulator computer and take the places of other incidents becoming familiar to trainees. The objective is not to catch them out but to teach every possibility.

By this stage crew members from flying school have progressed through OCU's Ground Training, Hercules Conversion, Hercules Training and Simulator Squadrons. 'Is there anything else they can learn,' one might ask, 'or more to the point, able to absorb?' Yet it is at this point that aircrew members are given that distinctive extra edge. It is accomplished by the last but not least part of OCU activities, the Support Training Squadron (STS) incorporating the Tanker Training Flight (TTF). These two specialist bodies are on 'C' Site at the south end of Lyneham airfield.

Support Training Squadron (STS) incorporating
Tanker Training Flight (TTF)

Hercules tanker and receiver aircraft. This picture was taken over the empty middle reaches of the South Atlantic. (Phil Fox)

The Support Training Squadron has two main responsibilities which are Air-to-Air Refuelling (AAR) and low flying/air dropping usually referred to as Transport Support (TS). It follows therefore that, in addition to Hercules tankers, Lyneham must maintain a standing force of tanker crews and receiver crews. Tanker crews form part of Nos 24 and 30 Squadrons only, while there are receiver crews in all four (24, 30 47 and 70) squadrons. To meet these

responsibilities, the Support Training Squadron provides the following tuition. Its Tanker Training Flight runs four 5-week tanker and five 2-week receiver courses a year. In the case of transport support (low flying/air dropping) there are five courses a year each of three crews. These latter 3-week courses are for training air loadmasters who then go on to five weeks of flying tuition. In all cases there are follow-up courses, either every six or twelve months to provide for standardisation, re-categorisation and to ensure peak efficiency.

The Tanker Training Flight is in an annexe to the main Support Training School. It contains all the publications, diagrams, equipment items and video tapes for preliminary classroom work. At RAF Lyneham there are six Hercules aircraft adapted as tankers. Each contains four 7000 lb fuel tanks in the hold: two abreast forward, a collector box in the centre and two abreast aft, with the hose drum unit fitted on the rear ramp. The refuelling pipe extends to 80 ft for pick-up, then pulls back to 40 ft during refuelling at 28-40psi. The system can transfer 10,000 lb of fuel in five minutes and the 28,000 lb is moved within a quarter of an

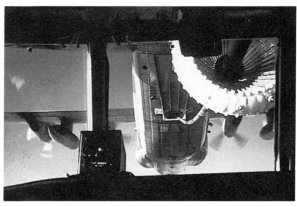

Above left: Pilot-eye view of the probe approaching the cone fitting at the end of an 80 ft hose from the tanker Hercules.

Above: Engagement has been made between probe and cone then 28,000 lb of fuel is exchanged within 15 minutes.

A view of engagement from the tanker aircraft. (Phil Fox)

hour. Break off pressure is 500 lb.

Such classroom work is necessary but not the final arbiter. Would-be tanker crews must show they can deliver, while receiver crews have to demonstrate the ability to connect with the refuelling hose on 50 separate occasions. These exercises commence in daylight and continue during the hours of darkness. Moreover, not only do they entail working with Hercules turboprop tankers, but also with jet-powered Victors and VC10s, as well as receiver Phantom fighters.

Overall, tanker aircrews go through the following training and operational sequences. After their initial conversion training, they do about 18 months' route flying in their squadrons before commencing specialist courses. After completing these courses they return to squadron duties, one of which entails a four month tour in the South Atlantic. There they fly Hercules tankers for Phantom fighters guarding the Falkland Islands. Before going to the South Atlantic, however, they take a further course, of two weeks, involving air drops to isolated islands and positions without airstrips. Additionally this further course covers fighter evasion techniques and survival in hostile environments which just about sums up life around that part of the world.

Turning now to the low flying/air dropping courses run by Support Training, these are arranged for Nos 47 and 70 Squadrons. They primarily affect 'C' Category crew members of which fifteen (three crews) attend at a time. The five-week course includes some 40-45 hours in the air. Again courses commence with classroom tuition. Low flying is mainly carried out to avoid detection by radar. It involves travelling below hill height and along valleys. As will be appreciated, flying among hills and in valleys has its hazards such as wind turbulence, sun dazzle and the hard hills themselves. Such difficulties are increased when using a large and heavy aircraft such as the Hercules which needs a mile across to turn through 180 degrees. Therefore low level route planning has to take careful account of wind strength, sun direction, successive hill heights and a host of other factors. To overlook one could be fatal.

Airborne exercises from Lyneham initially take place among the remoter valleys of Wales. They are carried out by three aircraft in Visual Tactical Formation (VTF) and exercises proceed towards airdropping as well as the low-level flying. Similarly, such operations take place in daylight as well as night-time conditions, the latter at heights averaging 1000 ft. At all times, trainee aircrews – although of operational squadron calibre – are accompanied by instructor aircrews.

In the third week of the low flying course, a formation of three aircraft (known as 'singletons') will move to an RAF station such as Lossiemouth and practise over the Scottish Highlands. It is not generally known that many service-minded landowners allow air drops on their estates and trainee crews use up to three different sites during any given sortie. They plan the whole air drop operation down to the last detail then often have the Support Training Squadron throw their plans 'out of kilter' (to use a Scottish expression) by introducing time, route and place changes.

The fourth week is taken up with formation flying using Station Keeping Equipment (SKE). This electronic aid was introduced in 1984 and is mostly employed when carrying paratroopers so that the aircraft keep together and troops drop together. It is also a weather penetration aid permitting formation flying in cloud.

RAF Lyneham works mainly with the Army's 5th Airborne Brigade at Aldershot. The required number of Hercules, suitably equipped, deploy to a designated airfield where the paratroopers and their supplies are emplaned. Prior to a drop, the paratroopers take their positions, up to 46 on each side, leading to the two doors. When the command comes, they go through their respective doors at a rate of one per second which means they are staggered at half second intervals. It also means they land in lines of less than 300 yards and have swift access to any kit dropped.

'Kit' can cover a multitude of military requirements from inflatable rubber boats to

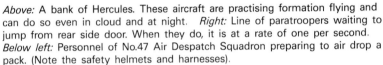

Above: A bank of Hercules. These aircraft are practising formation flying and can do so even in cloud and at night.   *Right:* Line of paratroopers waiting to jump from rear side door. When they do, it is at a rate of one per second.
Below left: Personnel of No.47 Air Despatch Squadron preparing to air drop a pack. (Note the safety helmets and harnesses).
Below right: The pack is pushed over the open rear ramp. Great care has to be taken not to slip on the floor rollers.

various types of vehicle. These are dropped by means of what are called wedges or in the case of heavy loads – like a field gun or a personnel carrier – with medium-stressed platforms (MSPs). A wedge is a structure mounted on the ramp, permitting kit to be dropped through a cargo door without the ramp being lowered. The wedge itself remains in the aircraft and is not dropped. This arrangement permits paratroops to jump from the side doors.

The medium-stressed platform is a base structure specifically designed to carry, say, a Land Rover and trailer for air dropping. The platform has an extractor chute to deploy the main chutes which pull it over the roller tracks on the Hercules hold floor, then out through the open ramp. The ramp and paratroop doors may not be opened simultaneously for reasons of structural strength. Thus it is not possible for one aircraft to carry both MSPs and paratroopers. The MSP is dropped on two 66 ft diameter main chutes and an auxiliary anti-swing chute, which carry and control the heavy load down to the ground.

47 AIR DESPATCH SQUADRON
ROYAL CORPS OF TRANSPORT

No 47 Air Despatch Squadron is part of the Army's RCT.

It will be appreciated that dropping heavy loads makes heavy demands on aircraft and aircrews. Briefly, the drill is as follows. The Navigator calls 'Red on' (five-second alert) then 'Green on'. As the parachutes are extracted by the slipstream, the loadmaster confirms 'Deployed' followed by 'Moving' after which the load leaves the hold; all of this happening within seconds. As for the captain, he has to take the aircraft smoothly through severe trim changes – also within seconds. When one experienced air-dropping pilot was asked the inevitable question, 'What does it feel like?' he thought for a moment before replying, 'Well, it *can* make your eyes water'.

Finally it must be mentioned that the training courses and methods described in this chapter by no means cover the entire range of activities carried out by Lyneham's No.242 Operational Conversion Unit. There are many other demands made on and met by this highly efficient training organisation. Adapting to change is an inherent fact of service life, as it is to tuition. Further facilities are being installed at No.242 OCU and long-term planning includes computerised techniques to improve training while reducing manpower and administrative costs.

Opposite top: An Ultra Low Level Airdrop (ULLA) of Lyneham Hercules at the moment of cargo extraction for an air drop.

Opposite bottom: A cluster of packs leave the ramp of a Hercules. (Photo by Adrian Balch)

Above: View from Hercules hold as Medium Stressed Platform (MSP) goes over end of ramp with parachutes already opening.

Left: Series of 1-ton containers with their parachutes just opening on leaving Hercules hold. Observer aircraft in foreground.

Chapter 7
ENGINEERING WING

Lyneham personnel regard the station and their work from various viewpoints. Operations staff think in terms of tasks – some routine, others out of the ordinary, all to be done well. Aircrews show an affection for the aircraft they fly. The Hercules may not have the elan of a Hawk or the raw power of a Tornado yet is regarded as a good working companion. When one crosses from air to ground crew a different set of values become evident and lead to another way of viewing RAF Lyneham.

On speaking to a Lyneham engineer about the obvious difficulty of looking after 60 Hercules, his reply was typical 'Sixty-one to be precise'. There was a slight pause then he added, 'In seven variants'. The engineer went on to stress the concern of all those who strive to keep machines serviceable, be they cars, trains, ships or aircraft. 'Here,' he said, 'we have to look after a corporate fleet that is used to the full. As you know, the Hercules at Lyneham are constantly in the air, year in, year out, route flying, freight carrying, air dropping, tanking, operating in remote areas, landing on the roughest of airstrips. It all goes to make the engineers' task very demanding.'

To meet these demands, Lyneham's Engineering Wing of approximately 1500 staff, including civilians, is organised in seven squadrons as follows:

Engineering Operations Squadron
A-Line Servicing Squadron
B-Line Servicing Squadron
Aircraft Engineering Squadron
Mechanical Engineering Squadron
Electrical Engineering Squadron
Mechanical Transport Squadron

Like other Lyneham wings, the work of individual squadrons, flights and sections are closely interconnected, not only within the wing but also with the rest of the station. In order to understand how the wing works, however, it will be described as listed.

Engineering Operations Squadron

This squadron is sited at the Lyneham Air Terminal close to and also inside the Operations Room. Its prime activities, called Eng. Plans and Eng. Ops, take the form of planning and co-ordinating engineering activities with those of flying operations. Thus all information from the other wing squadrons are channelled to meet airborne demands.

Starting with Eng. Plans, early every morning the programme for the next day's flying is analysed and available aircraft selected to suit the forthcoming tasks. An engineering plan is next produced and issued to everyone concerned, especially to ground crews who will work all that day and often into the night to have the designated aircraft ready for flying. At the same time Eng. Ops, whose personnel are always on duty in the Operations Room, will monitor aircraft states and provide advice on engineering aspects. They effectively control all the resources of Engineering Wing from servicing and rectification states to the positioning of aircraft and the delivery of its fuel.

Eng. Ops attendance in the Air Terminal Operations Room is made up of a Flight Sergeant and a Chief Technician. Both these NCOs carry the full authority of the Officer Commanding Engineering Wing whose office is in the same corridor. They are responsible for minute-to-minute decisions on all technical matters. Their jobs call for in-depth engineering knowledge gained from extensive experience of the maintenance lines, swift yet cool thinking and, above all, an ability to work with senior aircrew officers often during stressful sequence of events. They have to know the exact serviceability state of every RAF Hercules, not only at Lyneham, but throughout the world, together with the availability of all ancillary equipment and motor transport.

Many examples could be given though perhaps a humanitarian one, which took place while the writer was present, would serve best. A technician from the Engineering Wing was with a Hercules aircraft in Norway. Suddenly word came through of his mother's becoming seriously ill and being taken to a hospital in Devon. Immediate arrangements were made, not only to fly him back to Lyneham but also to get him directly to his mother's bedside. It all happened quickly and quietly with no drama made out of a crisis.

A- and B-Line Servicing Squadrons

These two servicing squadrons are located in two large hangars beyond the Air Terminal and next to the aircraft parking area known as the 'pan'. Together they carry out the multifarious maintenance tasks, necessary to keep the Lyneham Hercules fleet flying (other

A Hercules being towed out of the Line Servicing hangar after undergoing maintenance.

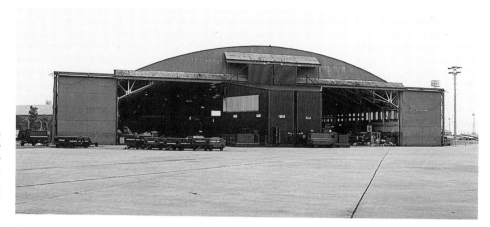

A view of the Line
Servicing hangar
showing the door
extensions which allow
three Hercules to be
accommodated at a
time.

than minor and major scheduled overhauls, to be dealt with later). Each squadron is made up of about 250 technicians in airframe, propulsion, electrical and avionic trades. For allocation of duties, squadrons are divided into flights whose members work a 12-hour day – four days on and four days off – swapping over at six in the evening. In the main, their duties consist of primary servicing and the rectification of reported defects either on the airfield or within the hangar.

An average engineering day at Lyneham consists of looking at aircraft on the flying plan, repairing faults discovered by aircrew prior to flight, refuelling and parking. At night the emphasis changes. This is the time when the majority of repairs are carried out and aircraft for flying next day are made ready. Each line has a support flight engaged on periodical servicing and repair jobs. A special feature of A-Line is its ability to operate away from Lyneham. Its teams possess field kit, tents, sleeping bags etc, for immediate deployment. As for B-Line, the 30 aircraft they look after include the tankers and, when it is visiting Lyneham, 'Snoopy' the long-nosed Hercules equipped to investigate weather conditions.

The role of the junior engineering officers on these lines is an interesting one. They come from universities or colleges of technology and, for their first 18 months, they are literally put 'in at the deep end'. They are, of course, supervised by senior engineers and even more so by long experienced NCOs. 'It is not a situation of issuing orders', said one such officer, 'but of observing, listening and learning.' Lessons learned include working hard and often living rough on detachment. To the question of 'Why do it when you can go into industry?' another junior engineering officer replied, 'Industry would not give me this much experience, in such depth, so soon'.

The word 'line' means maintaining aircraft on-line for flying. First-line or-level entails preparations for flight following the elimination of rectification work previously reported. Second-line servicing covers scheduled servicing, and third line further work to a deeper level. Fourth-line involves extensive overhaul usually by outside contractors. The initial servicing period on the Hercules – known as its Primary – occurs at four months or 400 flying hours, whichever comes soonest. Primaries are generally carried out at the weekends so as not to interfere with the working week – that is, if Lyneham can be said to have a normal working week.

Then, after twelve months or 1100 flying hours, the service is stepped up to a Minor involving much more work. Primaries or intermediate maintenance activities continue during the second year after which the aircraft undergoes what is called a Minor Star. For Majors, Lyneham Hercules go to Marshall of Cambridge where they are stripped down to their basic structures for thorough investigations. Primaries are carried out by the Line Servicing Squadrons and the Minors at the Aircraft Engineering Squadron (to be covered later in this Chapter).

Both A- and B-Line Servicing Squadron hangars are capable of taking three Hercules aircraft due to ingenious extension-type doors built on at each end. A typical hangar visit would show various kinds of servicing work in progress. The first aircraft might be on its primary; a second would have its wing tanks opened to install new fuel registering mechanisms; a third could be having old engine mounting bolts changed for new ones. Servicing is delegated and monitored from adjacent control rooms. Each room for A- and B-Line Servicing is run by eight key personnel. The team on duty consists of an engineering officer, three controllers and four trade technicians – all senior NCOs. The three controllers are:

Rectification Controller	Responsible for rectification of any fault occurring on the aircraft.
Preparation Controller	Responsible for all servicing, inspection before and replenishment after flight.
Documentation Controller	Responsible for the aircraft documents as is necessary when teams work shifts.

The four technicians are concerned with co-ordinating work done on the airframe, engines, electrics and avionics. They occupy desks adjacent to those of the controllers. Thus the controllers pass requirements to the technicians who, in turn, superintend work done by their respective teams.

Regarding the away teams, at the time of writing one such team was actually over the North Pole checking compasses. Later it went on to Anchorage in Alaska before returning to Lyneham. In addition, there are other away teams at Dakar, Belize and the Falklands. These are special teams distinct from A-Line technicians going abroad on their assignments. All are volunteers though only one in four are accepted for the particularly arduous tasks involved. They undergo four months' preliminary training followed by two months' advanced tuition, after which they stay with their team for four years.

Aircraft Engineering Squadron

This squadron, located in 'C' Site, employs some 260 personnel. Four of its teams carry out further periodic servicing to the aircraft known as Minors. These are much more detailed and thorough than those undertaken by the Line Servicing Squadrons. They inspect areas of the Hercules, normally inaccessible during day-to-day maintenance, also do any necessary repair work. As well as Minors, the Aircraft Engineering Squadron is responsible for servicing mechanical components which is done in corresponding bays. Additionally this squadron looks after the Hercules Maintenance School which teaches engineers of all ranks and trades about the finer points of this particular aircraft.

Visitors to RAF Lyneham, who are shown round the ever-busy hangars of A- and B-Line Servicing Squadrons and of Aircraft Engineering Squadron, may think that their duties are the same. Both take Hercules into their respective work areas and both have engineering teams, supervised from adjacent offices, working on them. However, as already stated, Aircraft Engineering has to cover more ground checks and in greater depth. This can be deduced from the network of safety scaffolding which almost hides the fuselage, mainplane, engines and even the high tail. Further evidence is provided by a tell-tale difference. Whereas most Hercules that receive general servicing rest normally on their tyres, those aircraft in Aircraft Engineering are jacked off the floor for landing gear checks.

Interior of the Air Engineering hangar with Hercules jacked off the floor for landing gear checks.

Work on a Hercules power plant. Note the abrasion marks on leading edges of propeller blades.

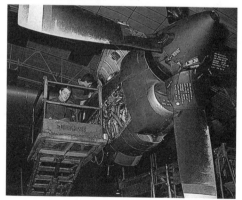

Aircraft Engineering Squadron personnel usually work days from 0800-1700 hours, though these often become 'extended days' with hours added to the beginning and end of shifts. On an average, Minor and Minor Star overhauls take twenty days. Much depends on what is found and how much has to be rectified. These very thorough overhauls follow rulebooks running into many volumes, from structures and engines, through controls and systems, to painting and finishing. After overhaul, every item and system is fully tested, first on the ground, then in the air.

The Hercules Maintenance School, provides a surprisingly wide range of courses on engineering aspects of the aircraft. Before a ground engineer can go anywhere near a Lyneham Hercules, he must attend and pass the necessary course. The basic course takes four months and it is followed by two months of close supervision 'on the lines'. Other courses of the maintenance school include a concentrated one for those personnel with managerial duties. While this book was being written, the incoming wing commander, in charge of engineering, was a pupil at the school learning or relearning like the rest.

Mechanical Engineering Squadron

This, the fifth squadron of the Engineering Wing, consists of three dissimilar flights. The first is located on the main central site, close to A- and B-Line Servicing, and the other two on 'C' and 'D' sites across the airfield. The three units are: 1) General Engineering Flight, which nominally looks after aircraft ground support gear but whose workshops serve the whole station, 2) Role and Survival Equipment Flight, attending to the numerous changes of Hercules hold fittings and life saving features; and 3) Propulsion Repair Flight, responsible for second-line overhauls of aircraft engines and propellers.

Starting with the General Engineering Flight, this is in turn sub-divided into two sections each very much dependent on the other. Its Ground Support Equipment Section maintains the multiplicity of mobile rigs and tackle used around the airfield and elsewhere. Its Station Workshop Section is there to assist GSE as well as everyone else.

There are over 1000 items of ground equipment such as generator sets, hydraulic trolleys, air compressors, space heaters, flood lights and lifting tackle at Lyneham. To give some idea of the quantities involved, the Ground Support Section looks after more than fifty 60 kVA generator sets and 300 variations of lifting gear. Compounding the problem, many of the items leave the station for temporary usage overseas. Others are purpose-built for permanent off-site working. For example the two sections – Ground Support and Station Workshops – built, operated and maintained a fuel blending plant sited at Dakar in support of Hercules tanker operations across the South Atlantic. Every ancillary must of necessity be kept in perfect running order. That entails regular servicing and overhauling which, in the case of the large diesels powering the generating sets, means stripping down to the crankshaft. As one engineer put it, 'There are no short cuts at Lyneham'.

The Station Workshops are housed in a small group of buildings where a surprisingly large variety of work is performed. There are well equipped bays for machining, welding, woodworking, metal forming, heat treatment and honest-to-goodness fitting. Work items seen in the shops give a good indication of their contribution to station activities. One sees instruction equipment and training aids for technical tuition. Stands for aircraft servicing are in the process of being repaired and rebuilt. Complex components are turned, milled and ground by the latest CNC machine tools to tight tolerances. Capability and adaptability are repeatedly demonstrated. 'We try to meet all station needs', another engineer said, 'and that includes the local Cheshire Home'.

The second flight of the Mechanical Engineering Squadron is concerned with Role and Survival Equipment. The Hercules can play over 50 roles such as air freighting, passenger carrying, load dropping and stretcher bearing. The equipment required to carry out each role is listed on a schedule, often accompanied by a loadmaster plan. Ranged round the RSE hangar are shelves and racks stocked with seat stanchions, roller panels, guidance beams, vehicle ramps, winch gear, even kennels for guard dogs. Working through their schedules, flight personnel count out the listed items – including all fastening, clips, nuts, bolts and washers – down to the last line and item. Loads are placed on pallets or in wire mesh baskets by the hangar doors and rechecked

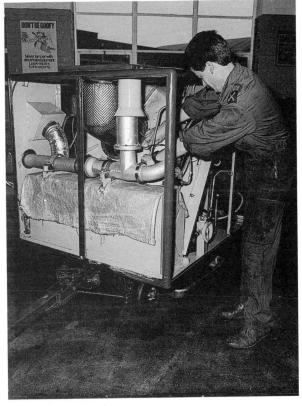

A technician of Mechanical Engineering Squadron repairing ground support equipment in workshop.

before being taken to the aircraft awaiting them. Then comes the long and heavy task of fitting which is why the flight runs a round-the-clock system.

The Propulsion Repair Flight further round the airfield is another world altogether. This unit has the heavy responsibility for overhauling and testing every engine powering the Hercules at RAF Lyneham. Currently there are 244 engines (four on each of the 61 aircraft) and a pool of 32 engines to keep the fleet flying. The latter might be regarded as quite a surplus until the facts of engineering life emerge. To begin with, six spare engines are kept at strategic sites around the world. Then there are the unserviceable engines; those being worked on and others awaiting attention or parts. The ever-changing situation is summed up by a multi-coloured wall chart confronting all concerned. The chart highlights the various engine states with (on nail-biting occasions) availability down to one.

Some 70 men and women forming the Propulsion Repair Flight strength perpetually strive to keep the pool of spare engines in two figures. Like much of the Engineering Wing they work days, extended days and when necessary through nights. Like other Lyneham personnel they can be and often are detached to remote places, eg, the Falklands (four months) or Ascension Island (six months). They go on courses to improve their technical skills and there are invariably other station duties to be performed. Effectively, therefore, the flight's work force averages 40 engineers. Between them, in the last two years, they refurbished 220 engines.

The Allison T56 turboprop engine powering the Hercules is made up of readily recognisable assemblies: compression, combustion and turbine. Together these drive a Hamilton Standard propeller through a reduction gearbox. These basic assemblies and their accessories are encapsulated in a modular frame called a quick engine change (QEC) unit. At the back of the QEC there is a bulkhead which matches one on the front of each airframe nacelle and to which the unit is secured by four stout bolts.

When in service, the engines and propellers are subjected to aerodynamic, thermodynamic and environmental extremes. Invariably assemblies are running a little too

An engineer of Propulsion Repair Flight working on a complete Quick Engine Change (QEC) unit.

Ground staff wearing protective clothing and working as a team to clean the entire aircraft.

hot or too cold, wearing here and there, revealing the onset of corrosion. It is the collective task of the ground engineers and repair flight specialists to pin-point these problems and to rectify them. In the words of one engineer, 'An engine is either fully serviceable or totally unserviceable. There can be no vague in-between areas'.

The Propulsion Repair Flight hangar is divided down its centre line. On one side are the serviceable powerplants in their QEC states ready to be installed on the next aircraft needing them. On the other side are those in work or awaiting parts for repair or replacement. Along the sides of the hangar are the usual specialist bays dealing with electrics, hydraulics, electro-hydraulics, propellers, their pitch-change control mechanisms and, significantly, an early failure detection centre. Another essential requirement is that of documentation. A test house is located nearby so that repaired engines, with their propellers, can be evaluated over the operational range. This extends from maximum forward revs in coarse pitch to those for reverse pitch.

Electrical Engineering Squadron

EES deals with all the electrical and electronic equipment at RAF Lyneham – in the air and on the ground. This squadron is divided into three flights: Avionics, Ground Radio and Simulator Servicing.

Interior of the Avionics Flight main workshop which is well lit, air-conditioned and spotlessly clean.

Avionics Flight is housed in a large modern building sited between the airfield and simulators. From its picture windows, Hercules aircraft can be seen smoothly taking off and landing thanks to the perfect functioning of their aircrews and their 'black boxes'. The centre is built round a large workshop that is well-lit, air-conditioned and spotlessly clean. Here all equipment is received, checked and, when necessary, rectified. The components are then rig tested to ensure that they meet their specification standards before being returned for aircraft usage. In-coming equipment covers units forwarded by the Hercules servicing squadrons as well as those coming from manufacturers.

The Ground Radio Flight (GRF) is predominantly concerned with the station's communications equipment. These units and systems range from relatively simple field telephones to highly complicated airfield radar and navigational beacons. The station telephone exchange and operators also come under the watchful eye of GRF which works with British Telecom who is responsible for such equipment. The Simulator Servicing Flight (SSF), looks after Lyneham's three high technology units. The simulators, as described in the previous chapter, are constantly in use and it requires a considerable engineering effort to keep them 100 per cent serviceable.

EES personnel work a normal day, but all are on call. It is not uncommon for technicians to have to concentrate on problem solving at four in the morning. As elsewhere at Lyneham, the work force is encouraged to submit ideas for improving efficiency and throughput. An incentive scheme is available yet there is more to it than that. Visitors are shown intricate test rigs, veritable works of electronics art, which technicians have constructed during their off-duty hours.

Mechanical Transport Squadron

Last but not least in the seven squadrons that go to make up Lyneham's Engineering Wing there is Mechanical Transport. This squadron is responsible for driving and maintaining some 350 vehicles of over 40 types. The fleet comprises those on the station strength and others from associated

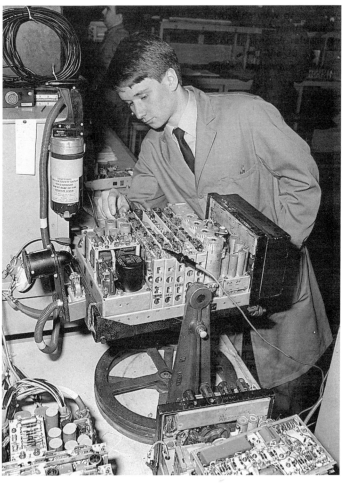

Work in progress on a 'black box' to ensure it is up to specification before return to aircraft usage.

service sections. Types range from Metro runabouts to heavy goods lorries, also specialised vehicles for such requirements as aircraft towing and snow blowing. To carry out airfield support, freight delivery, passenger ferrying and many other tasks, the squadron has 200 drivers including 60 civilians (mostly ex-RAF). There are also 50 motor engineers engaged on the never-ending work of keeping all vehicles serviceable. During an average year Lyneham motor transport – operating in, around and far from the base – cover $1\frac{1}{4}$ million miles.

Due to the vehicle mix and the variety of demands made, the Motor Transport Squadron works a four-shift system organised to include a permanent day team. Each shift has a senior NCO, two junior NCO's and twelve airmen to carry out allocated duties. Personnel come to the squadron mostly as Leading Aircraftmen and women from RAF driving school or as MT personel posted from other RAF stations as necessary. During the LACs first year they are restricted to Class 3 heavy goods vehicles (7.5 tons) and small coaches (14 seaters). This category includes the Metro runabouts and staff cars.

On becoming Senior Aircraftmen, the drivers go on a course for Class 2 heavy goods vehicles which also covers the handling of fuel tankers. Later, as corporals cleared to HGV1 standards, they can drive articulated lorries and trailers, mobile cranes, aircraft tugmasters and the other specialised vehicles operated by the squadron. As will be appreciated, it is vital to handle such vehicles with precision as the merest touch can do a great deal

Approach to one of
Lyneham's Motor
Transport hangars.
Lyneham has some 350
vehicles of over 40
types.

Engineering work
continues during flight
stops. Here personnel
carry out routine checks
at Kinloss.

of damage to aircraft. At all times, especially when reversing, the driver must have a colleague monitoring and controlling the exact position of the vehicle.

The Motor Transport Squadron at Lyneham is very much dispersed round the airfield. Its members claim that this is typical of most RAF stations where flying comes first and MT way down the list of priorities for the optimum central sites. Be that as it may, Lyneham seems to have evolved like the towns and villages around it. Thus the MT Air Cargo Section for loading aircraft is logically near the Air Terminal as is the Coach Pool on call from the Ops Rooms. The Maintenance Section lies quietly out of the way north at 'B' Site, MT Headquarters is located to the south at 'C' Site by the main road and the Air Support Flight on 'D' Site next to Air Traffic Control. These dispositions appear right in theory and, more important, work in practice.

Most interesting is the collection of specialist vehicles operated by Air Support Flight. Lined along the sides of the hangar – cleaned, serviced and ready for action – their tasks vary from routine to emergency. There are the massive aircraft refuellers with tank capacities of 4000 gallons, also capable of towing trailers containing a further 4000 gallons. There is the snow clearing equipment incorporating cutters, scrapers and blowers capable of removing falls from under six inches thick to over six feet high. One runway super-scraper, eighteen feet in width, was described as the best investment ever made by Lyneham. When asked why, it was pointed out that since purchase insufficient snow had fallen to warrant usage. Thus it stood, new and clean, as an ultimate deterrent to the weather.

Other vehicles lined along the hangar sides included freshwater bowsers, high access servicing platforms, runway sweepers and de-icing spreaders. Two materials are used to melt runway ice: polyglycol in temperatures down to -8°C and urea crystals for temperatures below that. Among the various vehicles and equipment there is an office cabin built to fit neatly into the hold of a Hercules and connect up with the aircraft's communication system. It was used when conveying the Prime Minister to the Falklands and is kept ready for other VIP occasions.

An Engineer Flight Sergeant in Operations Room dealing with Hercules fleet serviceability worldwide.

The work of the Motor Transport Squadron is so comprehensive and fragmented that it is difficult to convey the whole spectrum of activities. Its vehicles in and around Lyneham are on the move morning, noon and night. That is to be expected with a busy airfield. More revealing are the squadron's external though still regular duties. For example the MT squadron transports all aircraft equipment to and from manufacturers throughout South-West England. Their patch stretches from the Berkshire border across to Bristol and down to Plymouth. If something has to be moved, Lyneham moves it. The MT Squadron also ferries aircrews and ground crews, passengers and freight, is involved in all kinds of service exercises. A typical assignment was the first of many witnessed by the writer outside MT headquarters. A driver was checking the fastenings of a Hercules fuel tank on the back of his truck. When asked about the load and his journey, he said the tank had just been repaired by a Dorset firm and was now on its way to RAF Lossiemouth. 'I'm meeting the Lossiemouth people halfway,' the driver concluded by the door of his cab, 'at Carlisle. It's urgent.' It was also a midwinter evening.

This chapter is an attempt to shown the wide and varied activities of the Engineering Wing at Lyneham. As has been indicated, the overall organisational system and the individual working methods are all positively targeted. Engineers in particular, however, are always concerned with the negative side of their profession. They keep asking themselves silent questions like 'Have I missed anything?' or, 'Was I thorough enough?' Their constant doubts and fears were perhaps revealed in a text pinned to a hangar noticeboard. The words were 'Aviation in itself is not inherently dangerous, but it is terribly unforgiving of any carelessness, incapacity or neglect'.

Chapter 8
STATION
ADMINISTRATION

In the RAF, aircrew have been known to moan about groundcrew and groundcrew to groan about aircrew. They are, however, united in their views of administration: admin types, unquestionably, have the best of both worlds – wield power without responsibility, enjoy the good life. So why not eliminate administration at a stroke? The reasons why, as aircrew, groundcrew, and everyone else, well knows would be some large gaps. Gaps like pay and pensions, food and accommodation, medical attention and welfare. In fact, when one starts to study what administration covers – especially at a station the size of Lyneham – the variety and diversity of duties are impressive. They include:

Accommodation	Medical Care
Accounting	Messes and Clubs
Catering	Pay Points
Ceremonial	Personnel Services
Chaplains	Physical Education
Childrens Education	Police and Security
Civilian Administration	Postings
Community Relations	RAF Regiment
Dental Facilities	Resettlement
Duplicating	Savings and Insurance
Education and Training	Sports and Recreation
Estate Management	Station Services
Foreign Currencies	Travel Arrangements
Ground Defence	Typing Pool
Leaves	Welfare

It is not possible to do justice in a few pages to the span of administration which blends almost imperceptibly from official requirements, through education and training, to off-duty pastimes. So this chapter will concentrate on the more interesting official aspects while the next deals with general socially-related subjects. The units covered involve four squadrons (Personnel Services, Station Services, Accounts, Catering) and one flight (Police) as follows.

Personnel Services Squadron

The Personnel Services Squadron deals with pay, allowances, leaves, travel arrangements, postings and all the many other aspects applicable to everyone at Lyneham. Old-style pay parades no longer take place. Personnel are now credited directly into their bank accounts

Culmination of an Air Officer Commanding Parade, and proof of a well-run RAF station.

Lyneham's Administration Wing HQ responsible for the activities of some 10,000 people.

Medical and Dental Centre at Lyneham looking after the health of all personnel and their families.

confirmed by monthly statements. They can raise any queries either with their pay clerk or bank manager. For practical purposes, there is an alphabetical list of all personnel. Pay and documentation (PD) clerks are each responsible for 250 'customers'. The PD clerk telephone numbers are listed in the station directory so they may be called or visited. Again for practical purposes, people are advised to send memos which avoids unnecessary travelling about a spreadout station, and taking up too much telephone time.

The routine work of pay, allowances, leaves, postings, etc tends only to show the official face of Personnel Services. A great deal more goes on behind the scenes to try and do the best for Lyneham personnel. One example of this is the work done on welfare cases. Human problems do occur at all levels and, if the squadron can help, it will. Such problems often involve relatives and friends living elsewhere in the country, even overseas. If necessary these are visited in an attempt to solve the problem. The squadron has other organisations at its disposal to lend a helping hand. These include the Citizens Advice Bureau – the North Wiltshire branch for Lyneham which visits the base weekly – also the Soldiers', Sailors' and Airmen's Families Association (SSAFA). Many find it easier to talk to the Bureau or Association. They in turn have branches throughout the country. This good work is absolutely confidential.

Arranging leave is another important duty performed by Personnel Services. Airmen get 30 days' leave a year, Senior NCOs and officers 42. For leaves, all receive assisted travel to get them home and back to their station. Similarly, when they have to travel on official business – by car, train or plane – the service will meet such expenses.

Then, about every three years, many service personnel are posted which means not only travelling, but moving family and home. To smooth these moves is a 'package' which provides the many kinds of help available in these circumstances. It should also be mentioned that Lyneham differs from other stations in one important aspect. The presence of the RAF's tactical transport fleet at a single base makes necessary the presence of Hercules specialists who would be of much less value elsewhere. In practice, many key personnel tend to remain for several years at Lyneham.

For ease of handling, the Personnel Services Squadron is divided into four sections, covering legal, disciplinary, service and civilian personnel. All personnel problems falling into these categories are passed to the three officers and civilian administrator in charge. They have a difficult job, of which it could be said 'all human life is there'. Marital breakdowns, reconciliations, debt management, compassionate leaves; these are the daily tasks of the

Part of the extensive library in the Education Centre well stocked with books, papers, magazines and tapes.

PSS administrators. A current problem is finding good replacements for those civilians tempted away from Lyneham to nearby booming Swindon. The PSS has generated a programme of taking on part-timers, many of whom are ex-RAF men and women, also their service-minded relatives.

Accounts Squadron

Primarily this squadron deals with four main monetary areas: general accounts, allowances, sterling cash and currency exchanges. The first, for a station the size of Lyneham, is a huge task involving millions of pounds demanding detailed and complicated accountancy expertise. With regard to allowances, these are equally detailed and complicated to meet the thousands of claims submitted. The sterling cashier similarly deals with travel claims which, at Lyneham, run at around £$\frac{1}{2}$ million a month. As for currency exchanges, eight currencies are normally held to cover the requirements of most Hercules crews travelling overseas.

   An interesting matter is how these crews cope with expenses incurred as they continually fly all round the world. Their routes take them to advanced countries and less fortunate ones. Moreover, a sudden emergency can convert a simple flight of a few days into a detachment lasting several weeks. How do they pay to keep their Hercules running, and for their own needs? Money-wise, crew members set out on each trip with the travellers cheques and currencies deemed necessary for the planned journey, also a letter of authority enabling them, if necessary, to obtain more money en route. The letter of authority is held by the co-pilot who is responsible overall for money matters, thereby leaving the captain free to think about his aircraft, crew and task. The co-pilot therefore, deals with landing fees, handling charges, refuelling bills, crew accommodation, meals and the like. If in difficulty, he goes to the nearest British Embassy or Service base. Finally he has one card up his

Interior of Admin
General Office dealing
with a diversity of staff
support requirements.

sleeve. 'We find that this,' said one co-pilot holding up a not unknown piece of plastic, 'does very nicely, thank you'.

Catering Squadron

The third administration squadron to be considered here is that looking after the 'inner man'. Just as Napoleon I's Grand Army was reputed to march on its stomach, the Royal Air Force flies on theirs. The Catering Squadron comprises three messes – Officers, Sergeants and Junior Ranks – together with facilities to meet in-flight and passenger requirements. All food is bought in bulk from the NAAFI organisation, the Naval Victualling Department and local sources. Purchases are made for two-monthly messing periods amounting to over £100,000 per period. Approximately £45,000 worth of food stocks are held and these are issued twice a week to the three main messes and other sections. The average number of people fed at Lyneham three times a day is around 900, to which should be added extra meals for passengers. It is all done by three clerks, 24 stewards and 48 cooks.

The food store is simple and functional. It is stacked with bags, boxes and tins containing basic ingredients such as flour, fruit, vegetables, sugar, salt, tea, coffee, jams and preserves to quote only the obvious lines. One corner is reserved for Compo Rations used in field work. There are three variants of these providing sustenance for 10, 4 and 1 men over 24 hours. Nearby is the meat store with a walk-in freezer and several chest-type units, also a walk-in refrigerator. Fresh meat is delivered once a week then divided to meet mess requirements. The messes themselves could truly be compared to 5-, 4- and 3-star hotel restaurants. The most notable improvements have been made in the junior rank's mess as shall be covered later in this chapter.

Starting with Lyneham's Officers Mess, there are generally about 600 members, though they tend to come and go according to service demands. All those using the mess meals, refreshments and accommodation are billed monthly. The Lyneham Officers Mess is much more than an establishment for catering and the like. It is also the centre for VIP visits, civic functions, squadron reunions, receptions, dinners, dances and club nights. Its manager served in the RAF for three decades and has followed up by over 10 years looking after the mess. It has been honoured by Royal personages and the highest in the land.

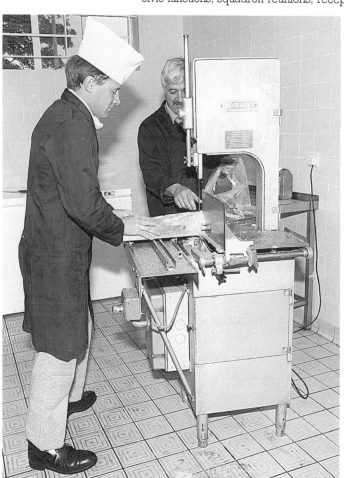

Fresh meat held in the store walk-in freezers being cut for delivery to the messes.

A tour of Lyneham's Officers Mess shows high traditional standards in décor, furnishing and service. The main dining room is noteworthy for its gleaming white linen, polished silver, sparkling cut glass, and quietly efficient service. There is a good choice of fine wines. As an alternative to the main dining room officers may go to another dining room for a swifter (and cheaper) meal. The same kind of choice is provided by two bars. There is the formal. bar where one has to be properly dressed, and what is called a 'scruffs bar', for those in flying or working clothes. Other amenities include a snooker room, library, sauna and squash court. One would have to search London for a better club. Officers staying at the mess have their own rooms with full facilities, and the area allocated to lady officers is most elegantly appointed. The establishment includes lock-up garages as an alternative to a spacious car park. The Officers Mess is self-accounting, providing its own improvements, as is the Sergeants Mess.

The Sergeants Mess is even larger than that for the officers having a membership of over 900 Senior NCO plus civilian ex-servicemen, totalling around 1000. About 125 live there, many on courses at Lyneham. Often there is an overspill when local hotels and guest houses are used. The mess feeds up to 150 people per meal. Its dining room is self-service and, like the Officers Mess, it has two bars for formal and informal usage. There are snooker and pool rooms, a sauna and a launderette. 'Sergeants,' as the guide said, 'like to get themselves organised.' This is very evident when walking round their mess. They have indulged themselves in fine wallpapers, fresh enamel paintwork, comfortable furniture, equipment for dances and discos. Large rooms open into yet larger rooms and one can easily visualise the succession of events and occasions enjoyed by all. 'When we add on the marquees,' the guide enthused, 'our guest list often exceeds 500.'

Starting at the top end of their entertainments programme, the sergeants organise three grand balls a year: Summer, Battle of Britain and Christmas. These are interspersed by squadron nights, ladies guest nights, parties with games and presents, parties for children, the disabled and old age pensioners, to quote only a few. The entertainers seem to get as much enjoyment out of these events as the entertained. They talk nostalgically of squadron reunions where 'still mad' veteran pilots try to fly from windows, and of other goings-on in the aptly named Romper Bar. Everyone has his story and preference, some surprising. 'What I like best,' said one sergeant, 'is having the Chelsea Pensioners. They come once a year and stay with us for a full fortnight. Marvellous chaps. Don't make them like that anymore.' Judging by their hosts, this might not be strictly correct.

The main surprise sprung by the changing Royal Air Force lay in the Junior Ranks Mess which, at Lyneham, is named the Wessex Restaurant. Gone are the long wooden tables scrubbed white and flanked by backless benches. Airmen no longer enter clutching 'irons' (knives, forks and spoons) and regulation mugs. As for the kitchens, where once those out of favour had to peel mountains of spuds or spend evenings up to the elbows in greasy washing up water, radical improvement has been wrought. Now all is stainless steel. Machines peel, grate and mix. Washing up is catered for by an inline unit with a conveyor

A typical Lyneham mess kitchen – all stainless steel, labour saving and to the highest standards of hygiene.

taking plates, cups glasses, cutlery and other utensils through hot sprays and warm air.

Each day about 650 Lyneham personnel use the Wessex Restaurant. This number is made up of people living-in on the station strength, those on duty, also service personnel passing through the base. The mess never closes though some periods are busier than others. Perhaps one should start describing the cycle when it comes properly to life at 0400 hours so as to be ready for first breakfasts around six. From then onwards, food preparation, cooking and servicing continue almost non-stop. Lunchtime is the busiest period and teatime the next busiest with hundreds of station personnel converging on the mess. Yet there is little crowding or waiting. The wide choice of food is ready and

waiting to be served. Night shifts are looked after by duty staff. About 150-200 shift personnel come in for hot food and drink between midnight and 0100 hours and sometimes breakfasts are served at three in the morning. During exercises, all ranks eat at the Wessex Restaurant and 2000 meals, additional to the norm, are not unknown.

The Junior Ranks Mess is built round a central food storage, preparation and cooking area. There is a production flow pattern through this area to two serving/eating sections. Even when the Wessex Restaurant was visited at a peak period (1300 hours), the kitchen and dining rooms were quiet. Behind the scenes, catering staff calmly attended to the gas-fired stoves and grills. In the dining rooms, personnel sat where they wished at cloth-covered tables for four with the meals of their choice. On one side was a fine display of cold salads, on the other dispensing machines for tea/coffee/chocolate/milk/squash/ice water. What about the food itself? Amazingly the main daily course offered 10 different dishes – a veritable Cordon Bleu selection. More amazingly, the chief at the Wessex said they provided three such superb meals at £1.18 a day.

He also mentioned that modern day airmen and women were very health conscious.

Exterior of the Wessex Restaurant for Junior Ranks providing a wide range of high quality meals.

Most ate properly and exercised regularly. To help them, the RAF tried to combine a carefully balanced diet with emphasis on high energy food. There is another factor which everyone knows and takes into account. The Junior Ranks are at the foot of the promotion ladder. With work and study, ability and application, the way up the ladder is open to all. No-one, however, no matter how worthy, will receive promotion if they are 25 per cent or more overweight. 'First and foremost,' said another catering NCO, 'service personnel must be fit. Literally fighting fit. We, the catering staff, the PT people and the medics all try to help. But in the end it is up to the individual.'

Police Flight

The RAF Police Flight at Lyneham likes to be regarded as a civilian police station serving a fair-sized town. It prefers to guide and co-ordinate, believing that the majority of modern day service personnel are sensible and responsible citizens in uniform. 'Nowadays,' its chief remarked, 'we tend to be advice givers, first-aiders, marriage counsellors and traffic wardens.' Nevertheless it is an imperfect world. The Police Flight has to investigate criminal offences, and safeguard aircraft, buildings, equipment and documents and, of course, people.

Likewise there are many other calls on the Police Flight such as processing passengers and their luggage through the Air Terminal. In the interest of safety everyone is searched before embarking on aircraft and their baggage has to go through an X-ray machine. Similarly the police check all incoming aircraft, especially the many foreign ones that land each

year at Lyneham. The Police Flight is
authorised by Customs and Excise (if
there is no C & E official available) to
meet inbound aircraft and carry out the
necessary clearance. These checks,
whether for inward or outward bound air
traffic, can take hours of police time.

The Police Flight maintains mobile
patrols of the station by day and night.
Patrols work within time frames designed
to give maximum coverage. By night or
in bad weather when visibility is
reduced, the men are augmented by
guard dogs. The RAF Police has long
recognised the natural abilities of
German Shepherds noted for keen
sense, strength and courage. Guard dogs
and their handlers usually operate during
the dark hours. Primarily they cover aircraft areas though all sites are visited.
Ideally a dog should patrol an area
devoid of people thereby allowing its full
potential for detection to be put into
effect. In reality the dog has to differentiate between ground staff and any
intruders, but the German Shepherd still
serves as an effective deterrent. The RAF
system is to have one man responsible
for one dog. In addition to their patrol
activities, the handling teams carry out
training exercises three times a week. If
a handler is posted overseas, the dog is
returned to the RAF school for retraining
with a new handler, just as his old master
teams up with a new dog at the overseas base.

There are two other, less visible, areas
of Lyneham police work covering Special Investigation (SI) and Counter Intelligence (CI).
The first is broadly equivalent to that of its CID counterpart. This section deals with matters
of a clearly criminal nature. It carries out preliminary investigations, collects evidence and
works closely with the civilian authorities. The responsibilities of the CI Section can be divided
into three aspects: countering the threats of sabotage, espionage and general subversion.
These aspects are in turn broken down into specific tasks – a safety net of checks and cross-
checks – to detect, then prevent any lapses in station security.

Police dog and handler.
The RAF has long
recognised the courage
and intelligence of
German Shepherd dogs.

Station Services Squadron

This squadron is the most diverse and widespread of those in the Administration Wing.
It literally covers the station and beyond. Its main activities include the organising and
administering of the station estates including the singles barracks and married quarters,
the RAF Regiment and Royal Auxiliary Air Force contingents on the base, and sports and
social activities. Also it has overall control of such services as typing, duplicating,

Another Admin aspect associated with dogs – Catering Squadron's £500 cheque raised and given to Guide Dogs for the Blind.

book-keeping and general duties. In keeping with the high standards set throughout the base, this squadron is a very professional organisation comparable with, if not exceeding, its equivalent in civilian life.

The squadron's major task lies in managing the estate that is Lyneham, namely, 2500 acres on which there are some 690 buildings and 800 married quarters, together with grasslands, roads and runways. Of accommodation alone, there are fourteen barrack blocks, twelve for airmen and two for airwomen. Of the 800 married quarters, 700 are for NCOs and Junior Ranks, 100 for Officers. The trend in today's Air Force, particularly in a base like Lyneham, is towards personnel buying their own homes. Thus the Wiltshire towns, villages and countryside surrounding the air base contain many more service personnel who, in turn, form part of the area's social fabric. Nevertheless, Lyneham constitutes a considerable estate and Station Services are there to manage it.

The barrack blocks for Junior Ranks reveal a significant shift away from the old-style rooms containing two rows of beds on which bedding was stacked in perfect order. An airman today has two keys: one to enter his building and another his own room. It is not a big room but each has a large window looking out on pleasant lawns and he is free to have what possessions he can fit into it. Family photographs, wild life posters, hi-fi and colour television with video recorders are the unsurprising artefacts that can turn a bare room into a home. Rooms are neat and tidy because they are inspected, yet the impression given is that of individuality.

Each barrack block usually houses 48 people, 24 at ground level and 24 on the first floor, The entrance hall and corridors are covered in highly polished vinyl tiles. At one end there is a washroom with hot and cold running water, at the other end a similar room with a washing machine and tumble drier. A common room is provided on both floors. Most service personnel have cars and these are kept either on open parks by the barrack blocks or in nearby closed garages. Next to the complex, stands the Pegasus Club for Junior Ranks and Corporals. The club has two bars, food machines and a battery of electronic games. It also enjoys the most modern disco centre in North Wiltshire that would be the envy of an expensive nightclub.

While this book was being produced, work on improving the Junior Ranks barrack blocks continues. Such work is inevitably subject to budgetary control, but the trend is towards better conditions. This is evident in the latest style of barrack blocks at Lyneham that are more like executive-style private houses. The first three – called Hercules, Halifax and

Hudson – stand in a picturesque corner near to Lyneham church. They are built of mellow-brick and contain the latest amenities. They are also clearly built to last and in the next century will blend in more with the village than the air base.

The same could be said of the married quarters ranged round the station's periphery. There are four different housing areas, their styles depending on when they were built. Lyneham's first married quarters was constructed in the mid-1940s, the last in the early 70s. The present position is that some 40 houses have become redundant due to service personnel buying their own homes further afield. Seven are currently used for other purposes such as for children playgroups. Different grades of houses are available either furnished or unfurnished. Occupants pay rents based on the grade of building and whether it is furnished. They also pay for gas/electricity. The Estates Office is responsible for maintaining the structural integrity of the property, the occupier its general interior. The latter is checked at the end of the stay and if damaged – eg, when a child or a pet has scratched or marked paintwork – an appropriate charge is made for redecoration.

It is interesting going round these estates. The neat brick-built houses stand amid lawns and among trees. There are detached and semi-detached properties of two, three and four bedrooms. On further observation, other aspects become evident. There are no gardens as such, just a climbing rose here and an ornamental bush there, as most people come and go within two or three years. The officers homes are distinguishable from those of other ranks by having garages beside the houses. The rest have their garages grouped at nearby sites. Plenty of parking areas are provided throughout the estates.

The estate roads have names associated with service aviation like Comet Close and Lancaster Square. On another estate called Slessor, there are Trenchard and Dickson Roads together with Portal Place. The officers married quarters lie, not separated from, but in the centre of other estates. Its roads are named after ducks: Teal Avenue, Sheld Drive, Pintail Court and Muscovy Close. In the centre of the officers estate there is the Station Commander's house next to a duckpond. So, in addition to his station responsibilities, the CO is duty bound to feed the ducks.

Grouped around him are the houses of those senior officers commanding the main wings of the station such as Operations, Engineering and Administration. This is not a cosy arrangement of all senior officers together. There is hard logic behind it. RAF Lyneham is operational day and night throughout the year. Sudden demands and emergencies come at all hours and have to be met with alacrity. It has not been unknown for the wing commanders concerned to hurry past the duck pond for an initial briefing in the early hours of the morning. Thereafter, instructions pass quickly down the line to squadron leaders and flight lieutenants, warrant officers and sergeants. Around the estates lights come on, car engines start up and alerted duty crews are augmented by back-up personnel for Lyneham's latest task.

Three other aspects of Station Services Squadron work should be mentioned here before going on to its more social activities. These are the RAF Regiment, Royal Auxiliary Air Force Defence Force and a small but vital area euphemistically called General Duties.

At Lyneham, the RAF Regiment constitutes a small group responsible for training all station personnel in ground

Group Captain John Bell presents cheques, totalling £4000 to local charities following a Senior Officers' 40-mile walk.

defence, weapons ability and tactical evaluation. Arrivals to the station spend up to four days learning about the base. After that they have annual refresher courses. Individuals are responsible for making the appointment and going on their refresher course which last one day. Even then, what with a host of other duties and commitments, some personnel find it hard to name the day and refer to the subject as the 'RAF regimen'.

The Royal Auxiliary Air Force Defence Force was formed recently to provide additional ground defence to Lyneham in times of national emergency. It consists of 100 personnel, all volunteers, who are prepared to train and work for a certain number of days a year. Membership is open to men and women from 17-50 (55 for ex-servicemen). Recruits receive free uniforms and are paid for days on duty.

Training comprises basic and specialist subjects aimed at supporting the main ground defence organisation. Examples are the guarding of key areas, control of entry points, first aid and fire fighting.

As for General Duties these – under the authoritative eye of the Station Warrant Officer – cover ceremonial occasions and disciplinary matters. RAF Lyneham maintains a Ceremonial Squadron of 60 men and 30 women drawn from throughout the base. These provide guards of honour for important visitors and make an equally brave showing on other official occasions such as at the station's annual inspection. Regarding discipline, this is concerned with general cleanliness around the base and airmanlike behaviour with ultimate deterrent of confinement in the guardroom.

As stated near the beginning of this chapter, administration blends almost imperceptibly from official requirements, through education and training, to off-duty pastimes. Official requirements have now been covered and the next chapter will progress through the very many social activities available to all those at Lyneham.

Chapter 9
SOCIAL ACTIVITIES

The title of this chapter may be defined as those activities which Lyneham personnel do voluntarily when off-duty. The range is vast – from academic subjects to sports, from acting to weight lifting. The Royal Air Force has always felt that, after demanding high on-duty standards, provision should be made to help pass the off-duty periods. More than any other service it provides an astonishing range of opportunities and facilities, all available, yet all voluntary. The aim is to create that difficult and almost indefinable advantage known as team spirit. Whether the RAF has succeeded in this worthy aim is left for the reader to judge by the end of the chapter.

To begin with academic qualifications, Lyneham has an Education and Training Centre for further education and extra training. It could be called a parallel opportunity for those wishing to better themselves. Personnel are free either to remain in their usual trade or to take advantage of an absolutely free, well-staffed and fully equipped further educational organisation. The centre provides a truly individual service tailored to the needs of each person so, as one education officer put it, 'If a person is keen, the success rate is high'.

The programmes of further education and training interface with colleges and universities. Initial tuition takes place at the centre to obtain standards and gain qualifications leading to higher courses. Classes are run in conjunction with local educational establishments. These are open, not only to service personnel, but also to dependants and civilians local to Lyneham. The next stage involves part-time courses in the required technical, commercial and cultural subjects at nearby Swindon and Chippenham, Bath and Bristol. Further afield there is a wide range of residential courses, held at leading universities, available to RAF personnel.

What sort of people take advantage of these opportunities? The short answer is all sorts. Some come merely to improve their basic English and communication skills. Others opt for maths or to learn more about the necessarily complex service documentation. Courses cover making applications, writing minutes, understanding forms, coping with rates and taxes. Junior ranks facing their promotion exams are given as much time and attention as officers about to run a squadron. As previously stated, those who are keen and persevere are rewarded. The Education and Training Centre is justly proud of achieving an average pass rate above 75 per cent.

There are many other services available at the Lyneham Centre for Education and Training. There is a large library of fiction, non-fiction and reference books available to service personnel, their families and civilian employees. Other books, especially those for reference, can be readily and quickly obtained.Daily papers, magazines and periodicals are laid out in pleasant surroundings. Another Centre opportunity is the lecture programme it organises throughout the year, particularly on winter evenings. Notable personages from

Swindon Air Training
Corps enthusiasts towing
Hercules 1000 ft to raise
£2500 towards a
squadron mini-bus.

A Hercules propeller
carefully restored by
Lyneham's engineers and
presented to the Calne
Air Training Corps.

Oxford, Cambridge, Government, industry and many professions come to talk about their specialised subjects. These lectures have proved very popular and are invariably well attended.

Two more aspects of Centre work for the young and the old, need to be mentioned. The RAF is well aware of the changes and upheavals which service children experience, and it tries to minimise the effects in every possible way. The Education Centre maintains close contact with the Wiltshire Education Authority, also with all local schools and colleges. Thus its staff is on the governing boards of most establishments. In Lyneham village there is an Infants School and a Junior School with a predominance of service children. In nearby Wootton Bassett there is a large Comprehensive School and the Lyneham children going there are ferried by education authority transport. There are also pre-school playgroups at Lyneham for service children between the ages of three and five years. At the other end of the age scale, the Centre caters for those about to terminate their service careers, either to retire or to enter business life. Resettlement counselling begins a full two years before exit and is repeated at six-monthly intervals. In the last year, the intervals become six-weekly ones to deal with all queries. Advice, training and help are made available. Even after leaving the service, close links can be maintained.

Education and academic training are activities in their own right. We now come back to a major part played by the Station Services Squadron, that of Physical Education.

Physical Education

There is truth in that old adage about 'all work and no play'. At Lyneham, the sports and social activities on offer are, to say the least, comprehensive. Taking sports first of all, here are 50 for a kick-off.

Angling (coarse)	Mountaineering	Equitation	Squash
Angling (sea)	Netball	Fencing	Sub-Aqua
Angling (game)	Orienteering	Football	Swimming
Archery	Parachuting	Gliding	Table Tennis
Athletics	Pentathlon	Golf	Ten-pin Bowling
Badminton	Rowing	Hang Gliding	Trampolining
Basketball	Rugby	Hockey	Triathlon
Body Building	Running	Judo	Volley Ball
Boxing	Sailing	Karate	Water Skiing
Canoeing	Shooting (small bore)	Keep Fit	Wind Surfing
Cricket	Shooting (rough)	Lawn Tennis	Weight Lifting
Cross-Country	Shooting (clay)	Motor Sports	Winter Sports
Cycling	Skiing		

With regard to the above, there has been a change in emphasis regarding service sporting activities, though the requirement for physical fitness remains the same. The change is that, while competitive sports are available, the main objective is to encourage and assist personnel to keep healthy through exercise irrespective of its nature. To this end, a Health and Exercise Lifestyle Programme (HELP) has been introduced. It is geared more towards assisting those who are overweight and generally out-of-condition. Some are referred by the Station Medical Officer. In practice, the majority decide to improve their own physical condition. It has been proved that personal motivation carries an individual through the course; there is no compulsion.

What happens when a person presents himself or herself at the Physical Education Centre and expresses a wish to become fitter and healthier? First there are some simple tests to decide what is needed. Next a schedule is devised tailored to requirements and time available. The schedule does not set unrealistic targets. It is based on how the body works, and people utilise self-knowledge for their own benefit. From the start, a one-to-one relationship is established between the Physical Education Instructor and the person setting out on the individually-devised course. Later, when fitter, the person can join in the lunchtime physical training sessions which have proved remarkably popular at Lyneham. Mondays and Wednesdays are for relative beginners, Tuesdays and Thursdays for the more advanced. In addition, the gymnasium is open every evening of the week with at least one instructor on duty. No civilian club could better these free facilities.

The centre for Lyneham's sports activities is its gymnasium, where there are squash courts, five tennis courts and six football fields. The gymnasium has a main 80x54 ft hall marked out and equipped for basketball, netball, volleyball and badminton. Off this hall are changing rooms, a weight training room, two of the three squash courts (the third is at the nearby Officers Mess), a sports store and an adventure or expeditions store.

The Sports Store holds the stations sports clothes and equipment. Round the wall-shelves are football, rugby, hockey and other garments in various team colours all washed and ready

Morris dancers in
Hercules hold dancing
their way up to 27,000 ft
and into the Guinness
Book of Records.

to wear at least twice a week. Resting in racks are bats, balls, rackets and wickets to quote only a few from a wide selection. Funding to buy sports clothes and gear comes from several sources, notably the MOD, service institutes and mess contributions. The upkeep of pitches, courts, clothes and sports equipment at Lyneham amount to about £16,000 a year.

The Adventure or Expeditions Store is an interesting adjunct to the sporting activities. It contains sufficient gear to equip teams of up to ten people. This equipment begins with such obvious requirements as tents and sleeping bags, cooking stoves and utensils, down to such vital details as tin openers. Ideas for expeditions of all kinds are welcome, though the RAF does make two provisos. First, each expedition has to be registered, after which the gear is booked out and has to be returned before the next venture. Secondly, each expedition has to be accompanied by a Qualified Adventure Instructor. This individual is not there to issue orders, but to advise and prevent the often foolish misadventures encountered by other organisations.

So far, the needs of individuals and small parties have been covered. The impression must not be given, however, that team games are becoming obsolete; the very opposite is the case. For those who enjoy team games, these are catered for in abundance. Lyneham teams play against each other as well as compete with other stations, other

One of the several sports
fields at RAF Lyneham
with part of the Married
Quarters in the
background.

Sports day. Runners compete for the many trophies and prizes presented by the station.

services, police, firemen and many civilian teams. Mention must be made of a major sports activity at Lyneham: the Station Commander's Trophy. This involves 16 teams from the various squadrons, flights and sections. The period covered is from January to December, which is another way of saying the whole year. The following list shows the scope of the competition.

January	Soccer and Table Tennis
February	Basketball
March	Hockey and Cross Country
April	Rugby and Volleyball
May	Netball and Shooting
June	Athletics and Dinghy Sailing
July	Cricket
August	Tennis and Golf
September	Squash
October	Badminton
November	Ten-Pin Bowling
December	Swimming

Each unit puts up the best possible teams to take it through the gruelling contest. There is a system of points awarded to the winning units over the year. WRAF teams receive bonus points for certain events though, watching them in action, this sexist advantage might well be queried. Every game for the Station Commander's Trophy has its rules set out clearly and is refereed by independent individuals. Outside events take place at the best local venues, eg, swimming at Calne's 25-metre pool and golf at the prestigious Malborough Club. Finally, to provide the best opportunity to excel, every event has a Sports Representative (usually an NCO) to ensure that all concerned get the best advice, coaching, equipment and, most important, encouragement available. Touring the Physical Education Centre and talking to crowds there – trainees as well as instructors – one meets tremendous enthusiasm for this part of Lyneham life.

The educational and physical training facilities described so far, cater for healthy minds and bodies. In addition, at Lyneham, there are plenty of hobbies and arts available to those so minded. These take the form of clubs for such activities as music making, model building, motor maintenance and live theatre. The station actually has its own theatre – the Juliana Goss – situated alongside the Pegasus Club. A very enthusiastic group welcomes all newcomers. Over the years the stage club has won many awards, both local and national. The Air Force itself holds a one-act play festival each year with many stations competing and it comes as no surprise that Lyneham consistently reaches the first three, and has achieved the top place. The Juliana Goss theatre seats 200 people in comfort, has a good size stage with a three-depth curtain system, fine sound and lighting facilities (thanks to RAF electricians),

Chelsea Pensioners regularly visit and stay at RAF Lyneham as Honoured Guests of the Sergeants Mess.

two dressing rooms and a props room. Its annual programme begins with a children's pantomine in January and continues with various one-act and three-act plays. Talks, lectures and concerts are also given there.

The activities described in the preceding chapter and this have followed a consistently progressive line from official administration, through semi-official areas such as education and training to hobbies and the arts. The next stage takes one into the fascinating world of community relations.

Community Relations

The service title Community Relations approximates to that of Public Relations in business, though with one significant difference. Whereas Public Relations are aimed at promoting company images and selling their products, Community Relations are intended more to inform and involve those living – in this case – around Lyneham. Community is the key word. Service personnel are drawn from other communities, are posted to the RAF Lyneham community then, with their families, put down roots in surrounding communities. Similarly local residents are curious both about the newcomers and what they are doing. Community Relations at Lyneham cover an impressive range of activities. Some may be obvious while others are surprising and even inspiring.

The Community Relations Office is charged with the twin tasks of informing and involving. The first is accomplished in conjunction with the media – namely, the press, radio and television. A two-way exchange of ideas is encouraged by as many visits between the community and the station as possible. By such means, a better understanding is reached by all concerned.For example, many RAF stations have to deal with the problem of aircraft noise. Fortunately for Lyneham the turboprop-powered Hercules is relatively quiet when compared with jet aircraft. Nevertheless the local community is informed in advance before any low flying, formation exercises or large scale operations take place. Moreover, if there is a complaint, it is immediately investigated and answered on a person-to-person basis.

Dealing with visits to Lyneham is much more complex. There are so many requests for

Iris Bartle and Squadron Leader Chris Bartle in the RAF production of Farquhar's 'The Recruiting Officer'. (Chris Bartle)

Olive Whitehead a founder member of the WRAF visiting Lyneham on her 90th birthday.

visits to the station that these have to be categorised then organised in great detail. Initial contacts are usually as a result of some meeting or a telephone call. However the contact is made, Lyneham always asks for confirmation in writing. In all cases the applicants receive replies either initiating the visit or providing a valid reason why the request cannot be met. Those accepted acquire serial numbers, become files, go on a visits register and are entered into the station diary. This may seem unduly bureaucratic until it is appreciated that Lyneham has over 2500 visitors a year. At the same time, the station has to carry on with routine duties which amount annually to:

Aircraft loaded and unloaded	3,000
Passenger movements handled	40,000
Take-offs and landings supervised	48,000
Hercules hours flown worldwide	49,000
Pounds weight of mail carried	356,000
Pounds weight of baggage conveyed	2,304,000
Pounds weight of freight transported	30,800,000

In the first week of the month preceding the visit, the relevant file is activated, escort officers nominated and squadrons advised. Nearer the day, programmes are prepared, escorts briefed, transport and catering arranged. These are for minor routine visits. Preparations increase for more official ones, civic visits and Royal occasions. When flying requirements are involved these have to fit into schedules already packed tight. A glance at the CRO's list of typical visits should indicate the organisation involved as well as the diversity.

Air Training Corps
Air Transport Association
Army Staff College
Borough Councils
Careers Officers
Diplomatic Corps
Foreign Services
Headmasters
Members of Parliament
Ministry of Defence
NATO
Parish Councils
Sixth Formers
Staff Colleges
Undergraduates
University Air Squadrons

Another Community Relations requirement is knowing and dealing with the media. This works like the wave effect when a pebble is thrown into a pool: from the centre outwards. The Community Relations Office invariably begins with the *Wootton Bassett Standard, Wiltshire Newspapers, Chippenham Times* plus local radio stations. If something big is taking place press, radio and television further afield, such as the *Western Daily Press* and HTV West, are alerted.For national coverage, contact is made via Strike Command or the Ministry of Defence. Often these preparations increase to a full-scale media visit.

A full-scale media visit usually involves running a coach (and advising the station police in case they keep stopping it). It requires passes, the agreement of key station personnel and having outside phones available for media usage. Journalists have been known to eat and drink so refreshments and the staff to serve them are further considerations. Another essential is the preparation of press packs giving details of the operation, captioned photographs, facts on the story and copies of speeches. News releases have to be accompanied by names of Lyneham contacts and their telephone numbers. The last two are vital when journalists, working to meet deadlines, want further items of information to complete their stories.

There are a host of other Lyneham Community Relations activities such as writing articles for local newspapers and aviation magazines, supplying photographs and meeting all kinds of requests. For example, the latter might range from sending a coloured sticker to a small child to arranging the scattering of a former serviceman's ashes; Then there are the requests from various organisations, schools and societies, which introduces another Community Relations activity, that of helping charities. Those supported by RAF Lyneham include:

Cheshire Homes
Childline
Children's Society
Day Care Centre, Freshbrook
Friends of Roundway Hospital, Swindon
Lease Hill Home for the Elderly, Swindon
Lord Dowding Sheltered Housing Project
Lyneham Day Care Centre
Meals on Wheels

National Deaf Childrens Society
Pinehurst Neighbours Centre, Swindon
Polish Air Force Association
Prospect Foundation
RAF Benevolent Fund
Redland Home for Mentally Handicapped
Samaritans
Save the Children Fund
Soldiers' Sailors' and Airmans' Families Association
St. John Ambulance

The support of charities does not mean that RAF Lyneham is located over a gold mine. The money has to be raised the hard way as the following examples should show.

Executives' Walk

This is a traditional Lyneham event for senior officers and their wives to give a shining example as well as to demonstrate their continuing fitness. Distances in the region of 40 miles are covered over such terrains as the Brecon Beacons. Sums raised exceed £4000. Traditionally also, the money is divided between four charities, three local and one RAF.

Charity Lift

A Lockheed C-130 Hercules aircraft weighs some 79,000 lb so a Lyneham sergeant decided to lift equivalent weights for charity inside an hour. Although much involved in contributing to good causes, this was the first time he had tried a sponsored lift. It was novel, attracted more sponsors than usual and everyone came to see if he could succeed. The sergeant succeeded and the money literally raised went towards buying a bus for a local home for mentally-handicapped adults.

Charity Cook

A Lyneham flight engineer, known as a 'Charity Dynamo' because he has packed more such work into his life and RAF career than most, decided to raise money towards restoration of the village/station church in a novel way. For twelve hours non-stop, in the church car park, he cooked and sold over 1000 take-away meals. People came from far and wide to buy them because his was not the usual fare on such occasions but exotic Chinese, Indian and Malayasian dishes.

Red Noses

During the Red Nose appeal for Oxfam, where all and sundry wore clowns noses as well as donating generously, Lyneham went one better. A red-nosed Hercules taxied up to the Air Terminal building flanked by suitably adorned fire engine and ambulance crews. After stopping and shutting down the engines the aircrew – each wearing a red hooter – emerged to meet the press and television. The resultant national coverage did much to promote this worthy cause.

GOSH Appeal

Swindon joined with Lyneham to raise funds for the £30 million Great Ormond Street Hospital (GOSH) National Appeal. The Mayor of Swindon suggested to the Lyneham Station

Commander that the event be launched by having a Hercules drop 2000 balloons over Swindon's Wyvern Theatre. The logistics of blowing up 2000 balloons and designing a tunnel for them to be forced through proved more of a challenge than arriving over the theatre at the exact moment of the civic occasion, but all was accomplished.

Hercules Cramming

Another bright idea for charity, which raised £1500, was sponsoring how many people could be crammed into the hold of a Hercules. It was suggested that, as the transport aircraft could carry 45,000 lb, it would be possible to cram into one 300 people weighing 150 lb on average. Lyneham got in 340 people witnessed by Mr Norris McWhirter of the *Guinness Book of Records*. A sum of £1000 went to the local Cheshire Home and the rest to ITV's Telethon.

The files in Lyneham's Community Relations Office are crammed with hundreds of such events. Most are commendable fund-raising ideas put into practice. Others stand out as being equally worthy though sometimes a trifle off-beat.

There was the story of a Corporal serving at a remote radar site on Mount Alice in the Falklands. Something he missed was the sight of an old-fashioned red telephone box. He wrote to the Chairman of British Telecom and after considerable 'community negotiations,' BT donated one and a crew from Lyneham's No.30 Squadron flew it to the Falklands. The telephone box is now connected and used. It is probably the most southerly British phone

340 RAF, ATC and Army personnel cramming a Hercules hold to raise £1500 for local Cheshire Home.

box in the world and is known affectionately as the Red Tardis.

Then there was the red fire engine. When the Hereford and Worcester Fire Brigade donated an 11-year-old (but perfectly serviceable) fire engine to the Harare Fire Brigade in Zimbabwe, the only problem remaining was that of getting it there. Once again Lyneham said 'Can do'. After loading it late one afternoon, the aircrew training flight Hercules left for Harare in the early hours of the following morning. The trainee crew, watched over by instructors, staged the aircraft through Akrotiri (2025 miles) and Nairobi (2410 miles) to arrive after flying a total of 5503 miles over 19 hours. Lyneham is happy to know that the fire engine is in service.

And there was the Lyneham airman promoted by a Soviet General. A Hercules was deployed to Odessa on a diplomatic mission. At the end of the stay, the British gave a small party for their Soviet hosts. As it happened, a technician was due for promotion that very day. General Victor Yeremin, Deputy Commander of the Ukraine Military District was asked if he would present the new badge. The Soviet General said he would be delighted to do so, thus notching up another Lyneham first: the first Chief Technician in the RAF to be promoted in the Soviet Union.

The Community Relations Office records every noteworthy item – newcomers, promotions, commendations, functions – for internal news sheets and external press releases. Summing up, it could be said that everyone at RAF Lyneham contributes to the excellent Community Relations enjoyed by the base.

Hercules about to airlift engine donated by Hereford and Worcester Brigade to fellow firemen in Zimbabwe.

Telephone box delivered by Lyneham Hercules for installation on Mount Alice on Falkland Island.

Chapter 10
LYNEHAM PERSONALITIES

Over a research period of several months during the preparation of this book dozens of people were interviewed.

The six individuals who are featured here are felt to be representative of those talked to and typical of today's Royal Air Force in general and Lyneham in particular.

John Smith

One could not begin with a better ordinary name than John Smith. Flight Lieutenant John Smith, Tasking Officer at Lyneham Air Plans, is, however, no ordinary person. John Smith's background is one of service for members of this Smith family have served their country – for well nigh 200 years. John himself joined the RAF in 1953 as a Halton apprentice and converted to aircrew in 1959 as an NCO Navigator. He navigated Valettas and Beverleys, followed by nine years with Britannias. Commissioned in 1971, John served as a Hercules Navigator for Nos 24 and 70 Squadrons. 'I have been to every country in the world,' he said in a matter-of-fact voice, 'except Japan and the South Pole.' 'What about the North Pole?' The question had to be asked. 'Oh I've been there,' John replied. 'Five times'.

John Smith flew in Valettas from the early to mid-sixties. Those flights were mostly around Europe and the Mediterranean. They were also slow with leisurely overnight stops. For example a trip to Gibraltar meant an enviable stopover in the South of France. During 1964 he converted to No.30 Squadron Beverleys – his favourite aircraft. These Beverley flights were longer; to Aden and Central Africa, even to the Far East. One historic flight took him to Hong Kong via Bahrain, Bombay, Calcutta, Bankok and Saigon. Due to delays, like three weeks' unserviceability in Thailand and reaching Vietnam during the Tet Offensive, the trip took three months. 'In those days,' John said, 'navigation was pre-historic. Done by a sextant. At least the Beverleys were so slow there was time to correct mistakes.'

In 1967, John joined No.99 Squadron at Lyneham flying Britannias. Every trip was long and interesting. The Britannias flew similar stage lengths as the Hercules, around 3000 miles. Distant places like Singapore and Hong Kong became regular runs. They were never dull, however, for the unexpected often happened. In Madagascar, for example, the island was hit by a tidal wave and it took three weeks to dry out the Britannia's electrics.

After serving four and a half years as an NCO Navigator, John Smith was commissioned. He moved to No.511 Squadron, first as a Flying Officer then a Flight Lieutenant, and helped bring the last Britannia back from the Far East by Christmas 1976. From 1978 onwards he served with Nos 24 and 70 Squadrons navigating Hercules. Inevitably, John was involved in the Falklands effort. He was asked: 'What was that like as a participant?' 'Superb!' he replied. 'I did more flying then than at any other time in my career. On five occasions

Flt Lt John Smith, Task Plans, at work using his extensive flying experience in the allocation of tasks to Lyneham squadrons.

John Smith displays the Wilkinson Sword of Peace awarded to RAF Lyneham for humane work in Ethiopia and the South Atlantic. (John Smith)

during the eighteen-month campaign, I broke the flying barrier of 100 hours a month.'

John Smith talked of airbridges as if these were a few steps in length. In reality the Falklands airbridge was a daunting 4600 nautical miles, mostly over empty ocean, with another 3000 miles needed for the supporting tanker. Throughout that year and a half, one airbridge a day was flown, after which requirements were reduced to four a month. In total some 650 airbridges were achieved by Lyneham Hercules and their crews. Apart from the superb flying, there must have been some drawbacks. 'Indeed,' John twirled his moustache, 'not enough home life'.

Turning to his five North Pole trips, John was asked why they went. 'To check navigation system gyros,' came the simple reply. The Hercules flew from Lyneham in pleasant Wiltshire to bleak Thule in North Greenland and from there across the Arctic. On reaching the pole, they did a few circuits, then headed home. 'In a straight line,' John explained, 'by following the Greenwich Meridian'. He made it sound like the proverbial 'piece of cake.'

We talked about RAF Lyneham. Was it different from other stations? If so, did he know why? John Smith had no

difficulty in answering. 'Lyneham's more of a permanent home,' he explained, 'as opposed to an average station. Air and ground crews tend to come here and stay. Ten to fifteen years.' Which he had done. Now Flight Lieutenant J. Smith, who has navigated aircraft to every country in the world (except Japan and the South Pole), uses his experience while allocating tasks to the four Lyneham Squadrons. The interview was punctuated by phone calls and people with queries. John answered them all without hesitation.

John is nearing retirement. What will he do then? His reply was typical of others at Lyneham. 'I have done a bit of work for The Shaftesbury Society, helping at nearby Burton Hill House School for physically handicapped children. This began when I was with No.24 Squadron. When you are working with those children, you soon stop seeing the disabilities. Instead you see a wonderful bunch of kids. In fact they help you rather than you them.' John Smith has already begun building other kinds of bridges.

Fred Taylor

Fred Taylor when he was Head Barman in the Officers Mess being presented to the Princess Royal.

Fred Taylor's home near Lyneham Post Office lies close to one end of the main runway. Every few minutes, a throttled-back Hercules, with flaps and landing gear extended, passes overhead. One soon ceases to notice the succession of aircraft though they sound reassuring to Fred Taylor as he attends to his fine garden and meticulously kept house. The latter is all the more commendable because Fred was left a widower some years ago. At the nearby station, person after person insisted that Fred must be interviewed. For he had been at Lyneham since its beginning, since in his own words 'the first little hut'. Now there is a veritable town, the growth of which Fred has witnessed over 40 years.

Fred was born at nearby Hilmarton, the last of twelve children. His father was a farm labourer working seven days a week for less than 30 shillings. When the weekly wage was brought home on Saturday evening, Fred's mother then walked the four miles to Calne for left-over meat at reduced prices. 'I wasn't too brilliant at school,' Fred said, 'and left at the usual 14.' He, too, began working on the farm, but gave that up during 1939 to help build Lyneham 'because the pay was better'. By June 1940 after the fall of France, 'when things began to look a bit desperate', Fred decided to enlist in the Royal Navy like one of his brothers. He travelled to Portsmouth and found the Navy full. The Marines, however, wanted construction workers and Fred joined them. While still in civilian clothes Fred's intake was reviewed by the King and Queen.

His service career as a Royal Marine took him to the North of Scotland and the Orkneys to build field quarters. It was a tough time. During the winter months, the wind never stopped and snow drifted over doors and windows. Suddenly after this punishing period, Fred was posted to Ceylon to help build a submarine base. But then his body rebelled, he went down with TB and was shipped back to England. He landed at Bristol and went straight into hospital. Twelve months later, in 1945, he was discharged from the Marines. Fred returned to Hilmarton and in 1946 started work as a civilian gardener at RAF Lyneham. Even then his health kept breaking down and eventually Fred was given a job as Steward in the Officers Mess.

Happily his health was improving because the job meant getting up at 0500 hours to start waking his officers at 0600 with cups of tea. After that came cleaning shoes, making beds, raking out and resetting the individual fireplaces enjoyed by the officers of those days. When the new mess was built, the RAF offered Fred the post of Head Barman at which he would excel until his retirement. Happily again, his health problems were over

Fred Taylor received no less than three AOC Commendations and the Imperial Service Medal.

for the new job started at 0700 hours and often went on after 0300 the following morning. There was stocktaking and book-keeping, but what Fred recalls most of all were the antics of high-spirited aircrews. It is difficult to select a couple of tales from the dozens he told.

'There was,' Fred related, 'a certain squadron that shall be nameless.' Its members constructed little cannons out of beer cans to fire tennis balls propelled by lighter fuel. The fun became so intense that the Station Commander had to order the entire squadron out of the mess. There was also the story of a retiring Station Commander. After a formal dinner, this personage had his shoes and socks removed following which the soles of his feet were covered with blacking. After that he was turned upside down, lifted and obliged to walk the entire length of the white ceiling. 'Were his footprints left there?' 'Well yes,' said Fred. 'That is until just before the next Royal visit.'

During his service over four decades, Fred Taylor was honoured to meet many Royals: the Queen and Prince Philip, Princess Margaret and the Princess Royal who, among her many duties, is also the Honorary Air Commodore of RAF Lyneham. Over these years, he received three AOC's commendations: in 1967 from Transport Command; in 1975 from No.46 Group; and in 1984 from Strike Command. In 1982, Fred was awarded the Imperial Service Medal. When his retirement came in May 1987, the RAF gave him 'a most marvellous send-off. First a car took Fred round the entire station to be greeted by all those he had served. This was followed by a top table lunch and, best of all, that afternoon, Fred had his very first flight in a Hercules, joining a training flight to the South Coast. Generous gifts were showered on him and individual squadrons invited him to separate parties. 'How do you fill your days now?' he was asked. 'Oh, I fill them all right,' Fred replied. 'Apart from my own family living nearby, RAF Lyneham is like another home to me where I am always welcome.'

Dawn Sharp

At RAF Lyneham, the WRAF contingent blends neatly into the life of the station. With quiet efficiency they carry out all manner of tasks. A WRAF officer controls expenditure totalling many millions of pounds. Another runs an engineering workshop, while others in overalls can be seen working in and around Hercules aircraft. Selecting and writing about a single individual is not fair on the rest, yet a WRAF personality must be included. The choice was handed back to the powers-that-be and, after much deliberation, Corporal Dawn Sharp of Mechanical Transport Squadron was named.

Corporal Dawn Sharp maintaining computer control of MT fleet movements on and off the air base.

Dawn radiates personality, friendliness and competence. Born at Stoke-on-Trent during

Dawn is trained to drive a wide range of service vehicles from light vans to heavy transporters.

the 1960s, Corporal Sharp recalls that, from the age of 11, she and three of her 'sports-mad friends' wanted to join the Physical Training side of the RAF. It comes as no surprise that she was the most determined and the only one actually to enlist – despite a Careers Officer saying there were no PT vacancies at that time. 'What have you then?' Dawn asked. 'Supplies, dog handling and driving,' he replied. 'I'd like the third,' said Dawn. 'At least I'll get about a bit.'

So in 1978 she went to Hereford for six weeks of basic training. 'Four left in the first week,' Dawn said 'and others did later.' But an Air Force career was what she had chosen and it was where she intended to succeed. Therefore Dawn learned to wear uniform, to parade correctly and, after passing out, was posted to St. Athan, near Barry. She had never driven before and the RAF proceeded to teach her how to manage just about every vehicle going. The MT course included 100 per cent knowledge of the Highway Code, to be proved by a written exam, also the passing of a civilian driving test at Cardiff. On-road tuition was thorough. Early each day, two trainees went out with an RAF instructor. One would drive all morning while the other sat in the back – so both absorbed the tuition – then the situation was reversed for the afternoon session. They drove on town streets and country lanes, along motorways and mountain roads. Even after passing her driving test, there were further exercises. One involved a closely monitored drive from St. Athan to RAF Innsworth, Gloucester, then back again – all in one night.

From St. Athan, Dawn was posted to the highly reputed RAF hospital at Ely, Cambridgeshire. There she drove ambulances on 'blue light' emergencies, also took patients all over the country. There likewise, Dawn met Graham Sharp, a Cook, and began going out with him. Both were due to be posted from Ely on the 3rd May 1983 with some leave due before their next posting. They married on the 7th May and came to Lyneham on the 14th where they lived in Married Quarters. When Dawn's husband was promoted and posted to nearby Brize Norton, they decided to buy their own home in between at Swindon. Thus each morning he sets off north-eastwards to the Cotswold Hills and she south-westwards to the Wiltshire Downs.

At Lyneham, Dawn works in the station MT Control room. Her duties include booking vehicles in and out, also overseeing their movements on and off camp. These detailed and constantly changing operations are computerised. The computer even does the paperwork, but it requires checking and confirming, programming and monitoring, to keep track of the very many transport tasks by day and night. Lyneham vehicles are continuously on the move from ferrying Hercules crews around the station to carrying loads to the far ends of the country. Dawn's day usually starts at 0800 hours and should end at 1700 hours though there are often extended days and turns at nightshift.

Despite her duties, Dawn Sharp is at Lyneham fulfilling the ambition she had from the age of eleven. Out of the 50 or more sports the station has on tap, she specialises in four of them: squash, table tennis, volleyball and hockey. In the fourth, Dawn is Captain of Lyneham's WRAF Hockey Team. Despite her trim size, there is no mistaking her enthusiasm and determination for the game. The appellation 'the gentle sex' no longer applies when Dawn wields a hockey stick.

She was asked to give her opinion of Lyneham from the woman's point of view. Being a forthright person, Dawn gave a direct answer. 'At some places, there are those who will only do what is required of them. Here at Lyneham people assist each other. They ask 'What's the problem? Can I help?' Corporal Dawn Sharp has 10 more years to go to complete the RAF's 22. One hopes the lights stay green for her. One suspects they will.

Flg Off Ian Hubert, in charge of a Servicing Flight, but learning all the time from more experienced staff.

Ian Hubert

People at Lyneham, especially those in the technical branches, often remarked that the role of a Junior Engineering Officer was a testing one. Engineering does not have the glamour of flying; it is dirty and difficult, yet carries heavy responsibilities. The young engineer, fresh from university and initial officer training, is put in charge of a 44-strong flight on one of the servicing lines. Whilst advice based on a wealth of knowledge and experience is readily available, he carries the technical, organisational and disciplinary cans. To examine this aspect, 24-year old Flying Officer Ian Hubert from Lyneham's B Line Servicing was selected.

Ian came from Chandlers Ford near Southampton where both his parents are teachers, his father a headmaster. He himself obtained eleven 'O'-and four 'A'-Levels (Maths, Further Maths, Physics and Economics). At the age of 18, Ian went to Salford University to read Aeronautical Engineering. He graduated in 1986. In his final year, personnel people from industry and commerce began the usual shopping around for graduates. Ian Hubert, however, had already decided that the RAF was for him because the service would allow him to work directly with aircraft.

Ian doing what he likes best, working directly with his team to keep aircraft serviceable.

Having made his decision, what was it like in practice? Ian went to see his University Liaison Officer and, unlike the other graduates, only made one application: for the Royal Air Force. This led, in September 1986, to the Officer and Aircrew Selection centre at Biggin Hill where he spent two and a half days of exacting tests and interviews. There were aptitude and intelligence tests, personal interviews and medical examination; all in-depth and very thorough. On the second day, applicants worked and were assessed in groups. They were called upon to reason, argue cases and show leadership potential with problem solving. On the last day, there were hangar exercises where teams had to overcome a series of obstacles with each applicant taking it in turn to lead the team. After that the applicants went home and waited for word of the result.

Ian was accepted and arrived at Cranwell on the 1st February 1987 for three months. He admitted it was 'a testing time', perhaps because his family had no long-term service experience. 'It meant,' he said, 'a complete change in lifestyle and was highly demanding.' Nevertheless he graduated and was sent to HQ Strike Command as 'holding' – ie, not established but assisting in every way to gain service experience. After that he was sent back to Cranwell for six months' engineering training – the RAF way. This course primarily covered airframes, engines, electrics, electronics, avionics and weapons systems with additional management courses. 'It provided me,' he said, 'with the essential basic knowledge to carry out my first tour.'

His first tour was at Lyneham. Ian Hubert arrived in June 1988 and, like everyone else, first went to the Hercules Training School. He was then briefed in his new post by a Junior Engineering Officer who was off on detachment to Mount Pleasant air base in the Falklands. His predecessor left after a month and then Ian was in charge of a Hercules Servicing Flight, 'in at the deep end'. His world became one of four 12-hour days on duty and four off, though somehow he found himself working over Christmas and Easter. The work was exacting yet challenging, but precisely what he had always wanted to do. Top priority was on the management of aircraft programmes covering complex technical situations. He also had to deal with the personal problems of the 44 people in his team from advice on career matters to difficulties at home. His place of work is functional and unglamorous. Specialist technicians come and go as they deal with servicing requirements. Beyond this always-active area, there is the hangar containing the great bulks of Hercules aircraft on which work continues throughout the 24 hours.

So how does this Junior Engineering Officer view his present lifestyle? 'I knew what I wanted to do,' said Ian Hubert, 'to work directly on aircraft. My expectations have been met and surpassed. I get job satisfaction and even enjoy the pressure – though not necessarily at the time. Engineering work is of a kind that cannot be dropped, handed on to someone else and forgotten. We don't so much worry but keep at it – that applies to everyone – until we are all satisfied.'

Although most live out, Ian Hubert resides in the Officers Mess enjoying its social contacts. He would like to do four months, like his predecessor, in a small remote unit to test adaptability. And after first tour, followed by a second course of engineering training, what then? 'I would still like to work directly on aircraft,' Ian answered. The RAF has chosen well.

John Stappard

When all is said and done, it can be argued that the RAF is essentially about flying. Taking this argument to a logical conclusion, it can also be said that flying is about piloting. Those who plan and work to put an aircraft into the air, even those who form part of the aircrew, simply depend on the pilot. At RAF Lyneham, person after person said, 'The pilot you must interview is John Stappard'. They did this because by notching up 15,000 flying hours, nearly 10,000 of which were on Hercules and mostly instructing, he had become the pilots' pilot.

Squadron Leader Stappard is a friendly, quietly-spoken person who listens to questions then gives exact answers. He did not have to fumble for a single fact. A Northumberland man, he joined the RAF as a boy of 16 in 1945. After four weeks of basic engineering training at Halton, he went to Cranwell for three years where he specialised in radio and radar. At the end of his course, John applied for aircrew. He was to service airborne radar sets for two years at St. Athan and Benson until the call came for his aircrew training. This he completed in 1951 when he was commissioned.

There followed a period flying Mosquitos at Swindenby and Hornets in Hong Kong, after which he returned to Central Flying School to instruct on Vampires. In 1963, John converted to the Argosys of the then Transport Command and served for three years in Aden. In 1965, he came to

Squadron Leader John Stappard has notched up 15,000 flying hours, 10,000 of which are on Hercules.

the peak of his career. John was posted back to the UK and out to the USA to learn about and fly back an aircraft called the Lockheed C-130 Hercules.

'I took to the Hercules right away,' said John. 'It felt right – a big plane with the characteristics of a small plane. After six weeks of ground school, simulator and flying training, I brought one of the early Hercules back to the UK, also helped set up the initial training unit at Thorney Island. We trained six crews every three months. Our efforts contributed to the complex task of getting the RAF's Hercules fleet into squadron service.' John's own efforts involved instructing, examining and working at Singapore and Cyprus where part of the fleet was based. As he put it, 'eventually they all came home to Lyneham, as I did

John Stappard in his usual captain's seat taking a Lyneham Hercules down to the Southern Hemisphere. (J. Stappard)

in 1979.' At Lyneham, John joined the Hercules Conversion Squadron where for the next ten years he would train pilots and become involved in most major operations. Thus he has been instructing since 1955 and he is still doing so today.

With regard to flying training, John feels strongly about maintaining high standards. He will take endless trouble to improve trainee skills, but there are those he cannot pass. For example, such a person could have a flying record with the statement: 'Failed Hawk, but should cope more easily with the Hercules'. In John's experience, the reasons for failure on other types remanifest themselves on the Hercules. 'With the C-130,' he pointed out, 'it is not as simple as it first seems. The work load for a Hercules pilot is enormous. Responsibilities include a much larger aircraft, bigger crew, passengers and freight, also a series of welfare, accommodation and transportation duties after landing.'

During his ten years training Hercules pilots, John has joined in every major emergency operation including Belize, Falklands and Ethiopia. While taking troops to Belize he continued training a conversion crew during the operation. Throughout the Falklands Campaign, he exceeded the 120 flying hours a month limit 'until they raised it'. For Ethiopia famine relief, he helped ferry vitally needed replacement aircraft to Addis Ababa.

In April 1989, at the age of 60, Squadron Leader John Stappard was offered further RAF service teaching youngsters how to fly. He now runs an Air Experience flight at nearby Bristol – one of sixteen such units round the country – where young people obtain their first taste of flying in Chipmunks. They come from schools, colleges and universities, girls as well as boys. Those at Bristol are fortunate: they could hardly find a more patient flying instructor with a safer pair of hands.

'Apart from the flying training,' said John, 'I talk about job satisfaction, also the differences between civil and military aviation. With civil flying, one can too easily slip into a boring, repetitive routine. When flying for the RAF, every situation is different. Instead of forever going from Heathrow to Kennedy, or Luton to Majorca, service aircrew are off to new and exciting places such as Nepal, García Lorca, Montevideo, Ascension Island and Mexico City. The great advantage of the Hercules is that it can do the lot. The C-130 may not be as smart as a VC10 or as exciting as a Tornado, but it is quietly doing different tasks all the time – generally full up to the gunwales. It is a friendly aircraft, makes friends wherever it goes and this is evident at its home base Lyneham.' For someone to speak so enthusiastically after 40 years flying, the case is irrefutable and the defence rests.

John Bell

During the time that the author was researching this book, Group Captain John Bell was RAF Lyneham's Station Commander. Though his tour of duty is now at an end, John Bell typifies the sort of men who command the RAF's air stations, and upon whose shoulders responsibility rests for the operation of these large and complex establishments. What is he like? What is his job like? How does he meet and overcome day-to-day, indeed hour-to-hour, demands. To try and find out the answers to such questions, one has to begin by going back in time.

During World War II, John's father was with the Royal Engineers and his parents were stationed around the Middle East. John was born there in 1940. Rather fascinatingly this took place at the German Hospital, Jerusalem and he was then christened on Christmas Day. Evacuated with his mother and elder sister, John spent his first years in Southern Africa returning to the UK in 1944. The family settled at Nottingham where he was educated at grammar school. On leaving school in 1959, John emigrated to what was then Rhodesia. There he worked for the Government Audit Department which enabled him to travel to the many Government outposts and see something of the true tribes and real wilds of Africa. It could be claimed that this unorthodox upbringing helped to form a distinctive frame of mind.

It was in 1964, following a conversation with some RAF officers visiting Southern Africa, that John returned to the

Group Captain John Bell, Lyneham Station Commander at the time this book was being written. An OC's duties range from tough responsibilities to pleasant ones like welcoming the Citizens Advice Bureau to Lyneham.

UK to join the Royal Air Force. He trained as Navigator at Hullavington and Stradishall, following which he was posted to No.24 Squadron where he flew on Hastings. During one such flight, after a low level drop and a return to West Raynham in Norfolk, he was standing (quite contrary to regulations) behind the captain and co-pilot as the aircraft came into land. The signaller on the crew, Flight Sergeant Johnny Marks (a stickler for regulations), insisted John should sit down and strap in. It was good advice because, just as the Hastings touched down, a wheel axle broke causing the aircraft to slew across the airfield, finally ending up on its nose with the tail in the air.

John's RAF career has covered an unusually wide and varied range of activities. Summarizing, it included early conversion to the Hercules in 1967 with eighteen months on No.36 Squadron at Lyneham to follow. Then came a Staff Navigation Course at Manby and a posting to Thorney Island in 1969 where John continued as an Instructor on the Hercules Conversion Unit. In 1972 he took an advanced Aero Systems Course at Manby and again remained as an Instructor, this time with the College of Air Warfare. There followed work at Boscombe Down on the Jaguar and attendance at Staff College, Bracknell before returning to Lyneham as Chief Navigation Instructor. After that came command of No.30 Squadron, a key posting to SHAPE in Belgium and back once more to Lyneham as Station Commander.

Such a career contained many highlights. John particularly recalls his period in 1983 as Detachment Commander on Ascension Island during the Falklands Campaign and the pressure to keep the airbridge to the Falklands open. At 0610 hours precisely, just as daylight showed in the East, a Hercules freighter and two tankers had to set out across the South

John Bell presenting a polar bear to a team off on a Joint Services Expedition to Ellesmere Island.

Atlantic. Throughout the day the freighter headed south topped up by the two airborne tankers which returned to Ascension. Before the freighter reached its point of no return – sometimes only an hour's flight short of RAF Stanley – a decision had to be made in the light of forecast weather conditions, as to whether the freighter should refuel and proceed. 'These decisions,' said John, 'affected crews who were flying to the limits of their skills and that of the aircraft. No matter how many times we had to recall an aircraft, in the end the airbridge always got through. You can guess that I was especially proud to be back at Lyneham seven years later when the last Hercules airbridge, callsign ASCOT 4165, landed back at base on the 23rd March 1989. Surely our maintaining that scheduled airbridge, the only scheduled flight in the world sustained by air-to-air refuelling, should become part of aviation history.'

Then in 1985 there was the Ethiopian famine relief operation of which John Bell related an essential detail not previously mentioned by others at Lyneham. 'The limiting factor to the amount of food we could airdrop was not the grain supplies nor the aircraft to deliver them, but lack of enough baseboards for the airdrops. These boards had to be made in Cyprus and flown to Addis Ababa, in itself a major airlift problem.' It was an interesting aspect of planning. At this stage John Bell was eventually persuaded to talk about himself and the problems of command.

'Responsibility,' he said, 'may rest squarely on an individual commander's shoulders, but the process of command depends more on the collective view than the whim of an individual. It is important to assemble the experts and talk technically complex situations through with them. In the end, the modern-day commander is only as good as his staff and they, in turn, have to rely on their teams. One simply cannot pull rank and make arbitary unilateral decisions. My way of working is to try and guide – perhaps I should say navigate – everyone towards an optimum multilaterally-agreed solution to whatever problem has been discussed. When that decision has been made, it becomes my responsibility which of course I do accept.' Having on his own admission (like many serving officers in today's armed forces) no inherited tradition of command, how has he coped with the stresses involved? 'I never dwell on what might happen,' John Bell replied. 'Instead I take a day at a time – even an hour at a time – and try to put my best efforts into the given period. To work in this manner demands that one must be on top form; meaning fit and well.'

John Bell is a strong advocate of physical fitness as he finds it helps immeasurably towards mental fitness. He jogs and windsurfs among other sports, also he encourages everyone to avail themselves of the facilities Lyneham has to offer. After the basic necessity of fitness, his priorities are to share his staff's workload and to support them at all times. 'Also to be natural,' he said, 'and not put on an act.' Other necessities are an innate sense of humour and, last but not least, a strong home base.'

'My family,' John Bell concluded, 'has been wonderfully supportive. This proved a great help because I suppose I am by nature someone who enjoys the Service way of life and all its upheavals. It can be very tough on families and I thank mine again and again. I did not join the Air Force solely to fly or just to enjoy an interesting career, but to take what comes and make whatever improvement I could. My best times? Looking back, I would say I have had the greatest satisfaction from my tours as an Instructor, passing on what I have learned from others and with the benefit of added experience.'

Chapter 11
FLIGHT PREPARATIONS

While watching Hercules aircraft taking off for their various tasks, it may come as a surprise to learn that many flight preparations began as long as two years ago. It is an aeronautical paradox that, in order to respond swiftly and smoothly as Lyneham so often does, it is first necessary to have a thoroughly planned and functioning organisation. The chief responsibility for getting a succession of aircraft off on time and safely to their destinations, also for co-ordinating all the station's many contributions towards this end, devolves on the Operations Wing.

This chapter covers the work done by Ops to prepare for each and every flight. As they would be the first to admit, however, much depends on inputs from other wings, squadrons, flights, sections and even individuals. In the background there are not only many teams, but teams of teams, working towards flight dates. To quote only a few, there are catering

Hercules 197 landing at dawn on Lyneham main runway after overnight Transatlantic route flight.

staff preparing flight rations, drivers conveying air and ground staff about the base, storemen supplying parts essential for aircraft serviceability, clerks listing passengers, air despatchers preparing drop packs. Therefore, although the Operations Wing is primarily described here, mention will be made of other contributions to help illustrate the full picture of what is happening.

The work of Ops Wing may be broken down into six parts.

Air Plans
Meteorological Office
Air Traffic Control
Fire Service
Air Operations
Flight Planning

Air Plans

Air Plans, housed in Lyneham's terminal building next to the Operations Room, are responsible for advance preparations of Hercules flights up to 24 hours before take-off. As just stated, these plans can commence some two years beforehand because, not only do they have to meet RAF needs, they also have to include those of the Army, Royal Navy and other services. Planning so far ahead involves high level discussions at the Ministry of Defence in London and other departments of state such as the Foreign Office. Similarly NATO exercises take months to prepare. Often, two years is a short time for what has to be done. These advance preparations move forward month by month. Some make steady progress, others are amended or even discarded while more are put in their place.

Six weeks prior to the month in which the flights are due, Lyneham air planning and engineering staff attend a meeting at No.1 Group Upavon. This is called a Pre-Air Transport Allocation Conference (ATAC). The flying programme for the following month is confirmed then passed to MOD London for a second ATAC meeting. At the London meeting, the financial implications are quantified for authorisation, modification or cancellation. Afterwards the approved list is taken back to Lyneham for actioning. Air Plans then allocate tasks to the Lyneham Squadrons. The squadrons will in turn select crews for the tasks.

Seven days before the task date, Air Plans will have prepared a task diary. This will contain all relevant current details concerning the flight. These task diaries have blue hard-back covers with the task number displayed on the spine. Internally, ring binders retain copies of all task signals exchanged to date, routing details, engineering requirements and, if necessary, diplomatic clearances. Captains collect task diaries from Air Plans and take them to crew briefing. They then fill in requirements for fuel, transport and special items such as Arctic survival gear. The captains then hand over the diaries to Ops the day before departure.

Meteorological Office

Meanwhile the meteorological staff of Operations Wing are carrying out their non-stop duties for all flights including the one to be covered here. It is interesting to record that the first official weather observation for RAF Lyneham was made in 1942. The present Lyneham Met Office is made up of two sections. There is an Observation Section in the Air Traffic Control tower across the airfield and a Forecasting Section in the Air Terminal building. The observers maintain a constant watch on local weather conditions and make hourly reports. They, like other RAF stations, pass their observations on to the National Meteorological office at Bracknell. From Bracknell, weather forecasts are transmitted to interested countries all over the world. This collective information is also passed back to

Met Office Forecasting Section at Lyneham Air Terminal responsible for briefing air crews.

the station for use by Hercules crews.

The Lyneham Met Office issues a constant stream of data about local, national and international weather patterns. In its offices, fax machines are forever printing out charts while display units relay pressures, temperatures, wind strength and direction, rainfall, sleet and snow. At the touch of a button, the met men can learn of the temperature at Gander or wind strength over Ascension Island. Thus, the Lyneham Met Office provides three services: local weather conditions up to 40 miles round the base, conditions to be expected on route flights and documentation for those making those flights.

Two folders issued by the Lyneham Met Office typify the invaluable work done by this section. They are Route Weather Forecasts for pilots and navigators, and those for Low-Level Flight. These are computer-printed documents produced for any task or time and containing an amazing amount of information. Each folder begins with an explanation of the symbols and letters used. Then follow computer-drawn maps of the flight area, perhaps the North Atlantic or the European Continent. One map will show a forecast of surface pressures and fronts projected to a specified time. Another will depict flying hazards to note and avoid such as cloud formations or icing conditions. A third will delineate air turbulence with the line of maximum disturbance and its boundaries beyond which smooth flying can be expected. The low-flying folders contain even more detailed information as weather conditions below 10,000 ft are influenced by the terrain. Such technically sophisticated documents show how far the Met Office has advanced since designing its badge – the weathercock. Incidentally the Met staff are all civil servants.

The Approach Room in Air Traffic Control monitoring all air traffic within 40 miles of the station.

Air Traffic Control

The Air Traffic Control Squadron (ATC) of the Operations Wing is a major communications centre. It controls all aircraft within a 40-mile radius of Lyneham. This is done in two rooms called Approach and Visual. The Approach Room is a dark, quiet air-conditioned chamber within the lower floor of the control tower. There radar surveillance is used to maintain aircraft separation and to direct inbound planes towards the airfield. All aircraft, military or civil, nearing the 40-mile radius zone have to call Lyneham on a fixed radio frequency for clearance to cross. The base is classified as a Military Emergency Diversion Airfield (MEDA). This means that, apart from its own flying activities, it is on constant stand-by for any military aircraft with a problem wishing to land. Happily,

The Visual Room above the Approach Room, which communicates directly with pilots within sight of the airfield.

emergencies are not frequent.

Above the Approach Room is situated the more familiar Visual Control Room. When inbound aircraft are within sight of the airfield, they switch frequencies from that of the radar controller to allow communication with the visual controller. It is the latter's task to ensure that all runways and taxiways are kept unobstructed. He controls aircraft (and other vehicles) on the ground as well as in the sky. At Lyneham about 49,000 aircraft land or depart every year so air traffic control is an exacting business. The primary consideration of everyone concerned is safety. They must also know how to respond in an emergency and there are training drills for this. There is also the Fire Service unit sited alongside the control tower, though it does have other duties throughout the station.

Fire Service

Since 1961, The Fire Service at Lyneham has been manned by civilians. The unit is made up of 40 very well trained and dedicated men. Their main role is to provide fire cover for all aircraft on or around the base. They know every inch of the runways, taxiways and exit gateways. They can be called upon to tackle anything from a major disaster to a cat stuck up a tree. Their fire engines, known as crash combines, are high-speed vehicles fitted with the latest safety equipment. It need hardly be said that the Fire Service section at Lyneham is manned 24 hours a day throughout the year. Happily their days are spent maintaining vehicles and gear, also checking on station buildings and particularly extinguishers.

Many other units at Lyneham work in the background. These unsung heroes and heroines routinely help to get the Hercules aircraft into the air, receive them on their return and keep working towards maximum standards of safety, serviceability and efficiency. Keeping the fleet serviceable and equipped is a mammoth task in itself. Apart from the engineering side, covered earlier, there are supply requirements which need to be met. There are also the pre-flight loading activities which often take days before the aircraft is due to leave.

Fire Service Section beside ATC tower providing cover for all aircraft on and around the base.

Supply Squadron

Lyneham has one of the RAF's largest supply squadrons. It is a truism to say that this squadron's prime function is to keep the Hercules fleet flying. This it does by the safe storage and immediate availability of hundreds of thousands of items. In effect, it supports the four operational squadrons, the various training squadrons, the station generally plus all personnel based at Lyneham and their dependants. To accomplish this formidable task, the Supply Squadron is divided into two flights, these being the Stockholding Flight (SHF), and the Supply Control and Accounting Flight (SCAF). Supply Squadron staff in both flights work shifts to provide urgent items during the so-called 'silent hours'.

Part of the Supply Squadron Main Store, its prime function being to keep the Lyneham Hercules fleet flying.

The Stockholding Flight is made up of several sections that deal with the very varied range of Hercules and other equipment. On the engineering side alone there are some 40,000 assemblies containing millions of parts. These are stored in the squadron's main supply building beside A- and B-Line Servicing. Larger items, such as tyres and airframe parts, are housed in a separate hangar. Then there are the petrol, oil and lubricants store (POL) and the mobility supply store where fly-away packs containing tools and spares are available for maintenance crews working some distance from Lyneham; like in Nepal or the Sudan. For practical everyday purposes, the Stockholding Flight has seven stores within the Engineering Wing – that is, right next to the work areas. These stores are linked to Supply Squadron HQ by computer.

At Supply Squadron HQ, the Supply Control and Accounting Flight is in turn computer linked, not only to Lyneham and the surrounding area but also to other RAF stations and many outside contractors. This computer network is necessary to identify makers part numbers and to locate the whereabouts of such items in the shortest possible time. There is an old naval saying that 'for want of a nail, the ship was lost'. Converted to modern day technology the gland in an electro-hydraulic unit or an integrated circuit in the heart of a black box are just as vital. All such supplies have to be available, particularly on the run-up to flight preparation, as do specialist-prepared packs when despatches in flight are required.

47 Air Despatch Squadron RCT

The work carried out by this squadron has been touched upon previously. An interesting facet of the squadron is that it is an Army unit comprising two troops and a REME section. It is a small group of soldiers entirely surrounded by airmen, albeit friendly and grateful ones. 47 Air Despatch Squadron makes up those packs that have to be dropped, installs

United Kingdom Mobile Air Movements Squadron (UK MAMS) team loading a trailer into a Hercules hold.

them in the aircraft hold (in conjunction with the air loadmaster) and then sees to the actual despatching in flight. This, it should be pointed out, is no odd job. During an average year, the squadron will pack, load and air despatch up to 7 million pounds (over 3000 tons) of stores and equipment. Loads vary from single free-drop sacks to the complicated configurations required when dropping vehicles and the like with parachutes.

Above: No.47 Air Despatch Squadron RCT loading pallet pack. Note the support placed under Hercules ramp.

Originally, 47 Air Despatch Squadron, Royal Corps of Transport was 47 Company, Royal Army Service Corps formed at Aldershot in 1900. It saw active service throughout World War I and again during World War II. The latter included evacuation from Dunkirk followed by almost non-stop operations in Europe and the Middle East. During the post-war period, the Company saw further service in the Berlin Airlift, Cyprus, Borneo and Aden. Renamed 47 Air Despatch Squadron, Royal Corps of Transport, it moved to Lyneham in 1967. Since then the air despatches have helped in all the station's operations, major and minor. They made stalwart contributions to Himalayan and Ethiopian famine relief operations – receiving the Wilkinson Sword of Peace for the second in 1986 – and throughout the Falklands Campaign they literally performed miracles of assembling, packing, loading and air dropping.

Air Operations

It has now been shown how various Lyneham services, either backing or contributing directly to the flight tasks, function. Returning to the Operations Wing, it is grouped round what could be called the core of the air base, namely, the Operations Room. This room is not a particularly large one. Personnel on duty in it can speak to each other without raising their voices. Theirs is the task of overseeing each aircraft towards its time of take-off, then keeping track of that aircraft as it crosses oceans and continents. The complexities involved are compounded by the fact that up to 40 Hercules at any one time are moving around the globe. Some are merely practising low-level flying through Welsh mountain valleys or dropping equipment on Scottish moors. Others are on routine flights to RAF Germany, Akrotiri, Dakar or Ascension Island. Others still are approaching Gander or Singapore or Melbourne. Air Operations know the exact whereabouts of all Lyneham aircraft and will confirm arrival times at destination airfields.

As has been said, the Lyneham Operations Room is not large. On one side windows look towards the airfield and down on the pan to and from which aircraft taxi and park. The opposite wall of the Ops Room is taken up with display boards. These cover the key points of all aircraft that are currently operational and the display items are constantly kept up to date. Between the windows and the wall boards sit a group of officers, NCOs and other operations staff. They are responsible for different functions such as routing, parking, engineering and, of course, maintaining the displays. Their inter-related duties are easier to understand if listed separately as follows:

The Decision Maker. The Duty Operations Controller who sits at an elevated desk in the centre of the Ops Room.

Route	Input of task diaries in programme and assembly of crews pre-flight.
Non-route	Handling movements of non-route aircraft arrivals and departures.
Parking	Precise location of every aircraft together with its associated equipment.
Engineering	Serviceability of aircraft not only at Lyneham but throughout the world.
Displays	Updating visual displays as derived from plans, signals and recorded movements.

The Duty Operations Controller, sitting at an elevated desk in the centre of the room, is the decision maker. He oversees all activities and, in conjunction with his associates, monitors

A view from the Ops Controller's desk across the room which is busy 24 hours a day, 365 days a year.

every movement of aircraft and their crews. The Operations Room at Lyneham has a total staff of 25. Those on duty work twelve hours on and twelve hours off keeping a round-the-clock round-the-world watch over Lyneham's fleet of Hercules.

Represented in the Operations Room and in offices around it are air planning, flight planning, engineering and met office personnel. People come and go as do the aircraft outside. 'Due at 1536,' someone says in response to a query. The minutes pass and presently the same officer confirms 'Touch down'. Not long after the Hercules in question rolls on to the pan and nods to a stop. The propellers also stop, doors open, motor transport appears. The scene seems somewhat casual yet its very smoothness speaks of long experience and high efficiency.

Meanwhile in the Operations Room, staff continue to monitor other aircraft, to update the wall displays. The central position of this visual aid is occupied by those aircraft operating away from Lyneham. There are four main columns listing task numbers, crew captains, the aircraft they are flying and the route tracks. If an aircraft is in the air, a white arrow points upwards, if on the ground the arrow is horizontal.

Route tracking is maintained via a complex communications system. The aircraft itself always keeps in touch with Lyneham. It is also monitored by other service and civil stations many of whom routinely inform Lyneham. For example, as a Lyneham Hercules approaches, say, Canadian air space, the aircraft identifies itself and radar eyes will be kept on it. Air traffic controllers may be likened to an international family, the members of which keep each other well informed. A Hercules winging its way across the wastes of the North Atlantic may seem alone but it is of interest to controllers in Scotland, Iceland, Greenland and Canada.

Meanwhile, in the Operations Room at Lyneham, the next day's flights are being assessed. The task diaries are already in their slots by the room entrance. The task numbers, captains and routes are going up on a day-before display for transfer soon to the day itself. What of the actual aircraft for the task? Of necessity this is a late decision because of all the factors involved. The main one is the serviceability of each aircraft. It is the engineers, with their detailed knowledge of every Hercules in the Lyneham fleet who will allocate aircraft to the tasks. They use a system of technical assessments with built-in priorities, a process that can continue right up to availability deadlines. The engineering representative in the Operations Room is kept fully informed of these assessments. Indeed he often plays a major part in the final stages of the selection process.

The next days' flying programme has now been displayed, the aircraft allocated, the crews aware of and already preparing for the flight ahead. All crew members have their responsibilities, but what of the flight captain on whose shoulders the collective responsibility rests? Lyneham captains and crews take their duties not so much lightly as confidently.

Route tracking. From left to right the four columns list tasks, captains, aircraft and main route stopping places.

This is because they were chosen carefully and trained thoroughly. They seem to go through the required procedures, checks and cross-checks as if without a thought. However, as much thought has gone into the drills as into applying them. Each step is a logical one in the whole sequence. Training has shown the reasons and experience proved them.

The following account is an attempt to describe the planning processes a Hercules Captain has to make before setting out, for example, on an Atlantic crossing. His crew members, who, it must be repeated, have their own responsibilities, are mentioned but emphasis is on the captain as he proceeds with his flight planning.

Flight Planning

A squadron has been informed of the required task and a crew drawn up for it. The captain nominated generally has a preliminary talk with his crew. Some he may know well; it is likely that they have flown many times together. Others may be newcomers to the squadron. They may have to be helped as well as watched. They will have to prove themselves. In addition the captain has to inspire confidence, to be known as 'a safe pair of hands', to show leadership qualities.

The Flight Planning Room. The walls are covered in maps and every document needed to fly anywhere is available. Here the captain, co-pilot and navigator run through their respective responsibilities prior to flight.

At this preliminary meeting, the captain outlines the task and initiates arrangements. His co-pilot for example has to draw the necessary money from the station cashier and lodge it for safe keeping in the Operations Room's safe. The navigator will have to polish up his knowledge on that particular route. The air loadmaster may have to pay attention to some special load. Arrangements are made for motor transport to help get them to next day's rendezvous.

Moving on to the day of departure, let us say the aircraft is due to take off at the civilised time of 1000 hours. The crew will have been on site and reporting to each other at around 0730. The captain, co-pilot and navigator will make for the air terminal building while the flight engineer and air loadmaster will want to get out to the aircraft. The loadmaster will have spent some time at Load Control in Ops checking paperwork and load details before going to the aircraft, with the engineer, about two hours in advance of departure.

The captain's first call that morning is to go to the Ops Room for the task diary. The diary's contents are summarised on three forms also included in the diary: Task Summary, Aircrew Preparation and Aircraft Preparation. These forms cover route stages, payloads, clock times and spaces for flight records to quote only a few. It is at this stage that the Captain and crew learn of the aircraft they will be flying.

Here mention must be made of what is called a Jetplan obtained by Ops and passed to the Captain. This document represents the almost miraculous efficiency and speed of modern communications. Details of the aircraft and proposed flight are relayed via satellite to Lockheed's computer at Atlanta Georgia. As manufacturer of the Hercules, Lockheed has fed into its computer the performance parameters of the aircraft. The computer memory banks also contain the world air route structures and there are continuous inputs of world weathers. Therefore, when the Atlanta computer receives and accepts the Lyneham call, it absorbs the data and quickly does what electronics people call 'number crunching'. Then, back comes the captain's quickest route in terms of flying time and fuel consumption. The Lyneham printer chatters out the relevant information, recommending fuel weights, reserves, optimum cruising heights and speeds, stage distances and a host of other items that he can compare with his flight plan.

The crew's next move is from the Ops Room to the Met Office a few steps along the corridor. To begin with they will be given details of the weather over Lyneham as at the time of departure. They will also be given data on weather over a nearby alternative airfield in case the aircraft has to land there because of some emergency. Next will come stage by stage weather forecasts across the Atlantic with, again, conditions over en route airfields in Ireland, Scotland, Iceland or the Azores, depending on the Jetplan, in case of any diversions to alternative landings. The weather report, together with his flight and jet plans, gives the captain a good idea of what the trip will be like. Throughout the flight it is the responsibility of his navigator to check and note the actual conditions of cruising speeds, fuel consumption, stage lengths and every aspect of the weather. This includes recording while en route winds and temperatures at cruising level. During flight also, the co-pilot records weather at airfields nominated as possible diversions.

After visiting the Operations Room and the Met Office the captain, co-pilot and navigator go to Flight Planning in the same corridor. This is a large room with big square tables occupying most of the floor area. There are great maps on the walls, also long rows of filing cabinets and shelving. The Flight Planning Room contains further detailed items of information necessary for making the projected journey. It is the responsibility of the captain, together with his co-pilot and navigator, to collect all such data, as well as to study and discuss it in this room.

To this end, the captain will have a check list of what to collect. He is likely to start with Notices to Airmen (NOTAMs). These give up-to-date information about hazards or unusual circumstances that might affect their route. Such things include temporary unserviceability of navigation or landing aids, the activity status of Danger and Restricted areas, or non-availability of runways at airfields due to maintenance. Thus, at this stage, the captain may have to modify his intended route which might in turn require taking on extra fuel and other considerations.

After this discussion the three crew members will concentrate on their respective responsibilities. The captain will ring Air Traffic Control to check which runway is in use. He will then make his take-off calculations based on the latest factors of wind and temperature together with aircraft weight. If on European flights, he will be interested in 'slot times', that is those times when he is able to insert his aircraft into the heavy air traffic over the United Kingdom and especially around its boundaries. The co-pilot will be studying and perhaps rechecking the en route weather forecasts. He will note the weather broadcasting stations available to him during the forthcoming flight; notably when each bulletin is due. All this information is given in pocket books called RAF En Route Supplements (Red covered for British Isles and Atlantic, Blue for Europe, Green for Mediterranean). The navigator will be checking the flight and jet plans once again against the information available in the planning room. He will then commence preparation of his proposed Navigation Flight Plan with particular reference to speeds and heights with fuel readings at every stage. At this stage, time is running out minute by minute.

Yet there is much more to do. The crew must collect their Route Bag which is a hold-all containing reference books, forms and the like to be used on their journey. The bag is labelled with their task number and call sign. On the top inside is an inventory of its contents which has to be signed for after reading and checking. The staff of the Flight Planning Room is responsible for assembling all possible information but it is the crew's responsibility to ensure that what they take with them is both complete and up-to-date. Contained in the bag prepared by Flight Planning and checked by the crew will be Terminal Approach Procedures (TAPs) for all possible airfields en route, other procedures of radio services, high and low altitude charts, runway details and docking areas. The crew will also separately collect RAF charts and various logs from the shelves and filing cabinets in the Flight Planning Room.

Last-minute arrangements are now made. The captain checks through their assembled kits. The co-pilot draws their money from the Ops Room safe and rings motor transport for wheels to take them out to their aircraft. There the crew is fully united: the captain, co-pilot and navigator with the flight engineer and air loadmaster. The latter two report on serviceability states and load details. The 'load' may mean passengers with whom the captain will have a few words. At last he slips into the left hand seat. The rest of his crew are already at their flight positions. Flight planning has been completed. Pre-flight checks are about to begin.

Chapter 12
ROUTE FLIGHT

A casual visitor to RAF Lyneham, looking along the lines of Hercules, will find it hard to visualise the variety and multiplicity of tasks achieved by these aircraft and their crews. Day and night, throughout the year, year after year, Hercules are departing on a succession of routine and special duties. The extent of these flights range over the United Kingdom, reach out to Europe, the Mediterranean, Middle and Far East. Lyneham Hercules regularly cross oceans and continents to meet service demands. These are called Route Flights and this chapter is about one of them.

Route Flight 5062 has been months in preparation, but it effectively begins in the Flight Planning Room. There, two crews are carefully going over the procedures and calculations described in the opening chapter. One crew from No.24 Squadron is to carry out Route Flight 5062, the other is off to the American Mid-West on another mission.

I am introduced to some of the 5062 crew. The Captain is Flight Lieutenant Andy Roberts, the Co-Pilot Flying Officer Bill Moore and the Navigator Flight Lieutenant Huw Thomas. Accompanying them is their Squadron Commander, Wing Commander David Farquhar.

The flight planning process is not all cut and dried. Changes keep occurring even as the calculations are being made which test the adaptability of the crew. One passenger has dropped out and others have had changes to their plans. Moreover, improving weather conditions over the North Atlantic offer a direct flight to Gander, Newfoundland instead of via Keflavik, Iceland for refuelling. Final calculations are made and agreed all round. The exact amount of fuel to be taken aboard is ordered by telephone.

We are driven to Hercules 199 standing ready, loaded and fuelled where Master Air Loadmaster Don Ward and Air Engineer Sergeant Adrian Wilson have been working for some hours. All confer, then visually check the outside of the aircraft before taking up their stations for engine starting and running. This procedure goes without a hitch and Hercules 199, initially captained by David Farquhar, begins to taxi.

Hercules 199, whose huge hold is packed solid with men and supplies for Belize, lifts easily off the Lyneham runway. Over the aircraft intercom system, cross-talk proceeds matter of factly. Calls for 'gear up' and 'flaps up' are followed by appropriate actions. As in most aircraft, however, minor snags are detected, rectified or noted. For example the navigator reports having a little trouble with his Doppler system, one of several navaids, 'wanting to drift off'. There is a technical discussion at the end of which all agree to keep a cross-check on the equipment.

Meanwhile an unconcerned Hercules 199 continues to climb. It is ascending through a magnificent summer morning sky. The air around us is pristine. From 10,000 feet the Severn Bridge can be admired in every engineering detail. To starboard the Brecon Beacons look like crumpled pieces of paper. Early morning mists lying in the hollows melt as I watch them.

Bill Moore, the Co-Pilot, shows me the altimeter. We are already at 20,000 feet and still climbing. Now South West Wales is sliding below us, its land areas soon replaced by fretted coastline. Layers of stratus cloud shelve the horizon ahead. At 24,000 feet David Farquhar levels out the aircraft and eases it to cruising speed before handing over to Andy Roberts. The flight to Belize has truly begun.

Southern Ireland is swiftly crossed. Ahead the broad North Atlantic, as applied to aviators, is made up of five radio controlled zones: Shannon, Keflavik, New York, Santa Maria and Gander. Our route passing through these zones rises from a latitude of 50°N to one of 54°N before sinking back to 50°N at Gander. Thus we shall neatly curve round that part of Planet Earth.

On his map, Navigator, Huw Thomas, has just as neatly marked points at 20, 30, 40 and 50°W longitude. The availability of diversions in case of an emergency, is also noted. Emergencies can happen very quickly in the air so not only must Alternates have been selected as part of Flight Planning, but the status and availability of the nearest at any moment of the flight must be known.

Lyneham Hercules 199 taxying to runway for take-off on Route Flight 5062.

Don Ward the Loadmaster takes me to see his area of responsibility. It begins from Bulkhead 245, immediately behind the flight deck, and extends to the rear ramp of the tightly packed hold. Half the load consists of crates and boxes, all neatly labelled. They are stacked and netted, each net being pulled tight by tensioners.

The other half of the hold is occupied by a large van and its trailer full of equipment. Miscellaneous packages fill every spare space and these, too, are fixed in position. Along the narrow side-seating, which space is about all there is left of the hold, service personnel sit or lie, read or doze. They will remain there for many hours.

On such flights, there is, of course, for passengers and crew the 'loo' problem. Hercules aircraft do not deign to provide the privacy, let along the luxury, of airliners. Their basic facilities are to be found on the port side down aft. A curtain barely conceals the urinal tube and chemical can.

Another feature of the Hercules is that its hold becomes progressively colder as one moves aft. The loo position is cold enough, but the coldest spot is further on at the top end of the ramp where temperatures fall below zero. To the uninitiated this may appear a drawback, yet Hercules crews have long since done some lateral thinking on the subject. Thus the top end of the ramp has been known to act as a flying refrigerator keeping fruit fresh from the tropics and even salmon from Canada.

By now Hercules 199 is well out over the Atlantic. From a rock steady 24,000 feet the ocean is a barely distinguishable silvery blue surface. Some 10,000 feet below the aircraft, pale grey clouds drift. Some 10,000 feet above, a Boeing Jumbo heads for Shannon with four neatly-ruled contrails behind it. The 400 or so passengers aboard are blissfully unaware of a workaday Hercules travelling in the opposite direction.

Our aircraft is on automatic pilot. The crew in the flight deck relax a little. There is general conversation over the intercom. Nevertheless, trained eyes keep monitoring instruments, compasses and radar screens.

Professionalism also shows in small ways. For example, when paper cups containing a choice of tea, coffee or squash are handed round, people help each other almost unseeingly – without spilling a drop. The cups fit into holders beside the pilots and flight engineer, while a double cup is used over the navigator's desk in case of leakage.

The Kingdom of the Clouds, which only air crews are privileged to see in all its beauty, is never the same for very long. One moment we are surveying an aerial world of pure blues, at another the nose of the aircraft burrows through murky grey. A vast cloud plain is traversed toward high cloud mountains. The range ahead has snow peaks, snow slopes, even snow spumes blown as it were from topmost ledges.

The cloud mountains are passed. The cloud plain sinks then is mysteriously shredded and disappears. This time the entire kingdom is cerulean. Hercules 199 seems to be suspended within a blue sphere which looks serene and inviting until someone breaks the spell by remarking, 'It's minus thirty degrees outside'.

Inside, on Huw's route map, thirty degrees west is roughly Mid-Atlantic between Shannon and Gander, the critical point. Better to go on than back. At 40°W, as radio contact is made with Gander, Sunday lunch is served: steak, trifle, cheese and biscuits.

The meal is followed by Bill Moore's, as part of his Co-Pilot duties, handing out the crew's travel allowances in Canadian and American dollars. He carefully counts the dollar bills and makes each member sign for what is received. He also informs all concerned that next morning's early call will be at 0445 hours Canadian time. Tomorrow is going to be a long day.

Meanwhile, today's flight to Gander is nearing its end. Hercules 199 continues to fly sweetly and smoothly at 300 knots in the thin cold air of 24,000 feet. Inside, all is warm and comfortable. It is like being on a truck or train. The engines sound perfectly relaxed, giving an impression of effortless power. The propeller blades are translucent disks. It is difficult to appreciate the sequence of engine and propeller revolutions being converted to blade thrust, of air flowing over the mainplane aerofoil to achieve lift.

There is general admiration for the Hercules. As one crew member explains. 'Those Lockheed boys really got it right. When the time comes to design a replacement, it will need a spacious roll-on roll-off hold, a high tailplane to facilitate loading, and four generously powered turboprop engines – in fact, just like old Albert here.'

Gander air traffic control is talking to Hercules 199. The local weather conditions are said to be near perfect. Captain Andy Roberts enjoys a fine visual approach. He initiates the downward slide through 18,000 and 15,000 to 10,000 feet. At the last there are 30 miles to go before touchdown.

First stage of route flight completed with Hercules 199 parked facing Gander Air Terminal.

Gander Airport comes into sight amid stretches of fir forests, bare rocks, inland lakes blending with sea inlets. Control mentions a slight cross-wind as the slide nears the runway. Despite this, Andy's landing is featherlight. A short taxi run and 199 is parked cosily beside Lyneham's 201 which arrived an hour earlier on its way to the American Mid-West.

After looking after the first Lyneham crew to appear, Flight Lieutenant Fred Moffit, RAF Detachment Commander at Gander, is there to greet the second. The crew change from flying suits to No.2s (second best blues) in his outer office. He then whisks them through the airport to waiting taxis. Within five minutes, because Gander is not an overlarge town, the crew members are in their hotel rooms with a bottle of beer apiece, compliments of Fred Moffit. He has also laid on a barbecue for both crews and service passengers that evening.

Fred is about to end his tour of duty at Gander and return to Lyneham for further Hercules training. Did he find his time in Canada tedious? 'Not at all!' Fred scoffs at the very idea. 'Where else in the world can a keen fisherman, such as myself, buy a season's salmon fishing for ten dollars? And the best trout in the world are free. As for the lobsters . . .'

Sunday ends with the barbecue, a couple more beers and an early night.

At 0445 hours the crew and passengers of Hercules 199 assemble in the hotel lobby. On the way to the airport, someone explains that those who fly in Hercules aircraft do not suffer from jet lag, only prop flop.

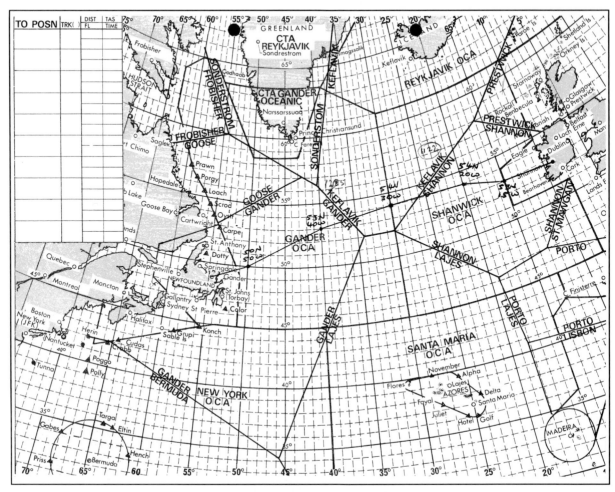

TO POSN	TRK( )	DIST		TAS	
		FL		TIME	

Captain of Aircraft Chart for the Lyneham to Gander leg of the jorney to Belize. The route is marked off in map references, the distance being 2338 miles.

The airport is crowded with Cubans about to board a plane for a Russian holiday. The RAF contingent moves purposefully through the crowds, crossing arrival and departure lounges via unlabelled doors, short cutting the system.

In Fred's outer office, flying kit is quickly donned. The engineer and loadmaster go directly to the aircraft, the pilots and navigator to flight planning. The latter carefully consult a thick volume of notices to airmen (NOTAMS), for today's flight is to Dulles International Airport at Washington DC and beyond, amidst some of the densest air traffic in the world.

During the day, therefore, pressure will build up on Captain Andy Roberts and Co-Pilot Bill Moore. Nevertheless, they work steadily on their flight plan with Navigator Huw Thomas and complete this within the one and a half hours allocated for the task. Then they go out to Hercules 199 for a half hour pre- flight check.

The engines are run-up and the aircraft begins to roll on schedule. Gander control confirms a wind speed of 24 knots and a cloud base of 2200 feet. Clearance for take-off is given and Hercules 199 soon lifts easily off the runway. It climbs just as smoothly through the clouds to reach a cruising level of 24,000 feet.

The Eastern Seaboard of North America passes below the aircraft. From Yarmouth at the southern tip of Nova Scotia, our route crosses the Gulf of Maine towards Boston, Massachusetts. Other good old English names crowd the charts – Weymouth, Worcester, Hampton and Hartford – to which are added good old Yankee names as Nashua, Nantucket and Martha's Vineyard.

It is here that the air traffic increases dramatically. The route map looks like a collection of spiders' webs because of the lines radiating from so many city and town airports. Flight paths to follow and levels to observe litter the page. Aboard Hercules 199, map after map is unfolded, scrutinized, then refolded. The flight deck is quiet as the two pilots concentrate and confer.

Clearance comes through for Hercules 199 to take an inland route parallel to Long Island Sound. The cities and towns below are bound, tighter and tighter, by roads, and knotted junctions. Visibility is near perfect. The sky looks empty, but the crew's headsets are crackling with American voices. These chatter in numbers, acronyms and occasional dry humour. 'One zero seven. Five miles.' – 'Attention, attention. late entry.' – 'Estimate Dulles fourteen miles.' – 'Let's have that again.' – 'Continue like the man said.' – 'Push through but maintain separation.'

Suddenly air traffic control refers to an unidentified contact. Immediately everyone on the Hercules flight deck begins peering through its many windows. They cease their observations and fall about laughing when a controller remarks, 'OK fellas, you can relax. It's only a truck.'

The unknown truck, whose radio is causing this aerial intrusion, continues its earthbound way. The Hercules sinks towards the green forests and red fields of Virginia. Below 10,000 feet, other aircraft are visible landing and taking off, circling and stacking over Dulles.

The Lyneham Hercules is fortunate. Air traffic gives 199 an immediate entry. Andy Roberts

Below left: Landing approach to Dulles International Airport, Washing DC. Note the tyre marks on the runway.

Below: Taxying to the airport parking area past the distinctive Dulles terminal building and tower.

Immediately the aircraft is parked a mobile generator is plugged in to provide ground power.

Air Engineer Adrian Wilson goes topside of Hercules to carry out engine checks during short stopover.

begins his approach and the runway rapidly seems to rise. There is a short strip of black tyre marks on the runway and the Hercules tyres add to it. Within seconds, reverse propeller pitch is applied bringing the heavily laden aircraft to a smooth halt.

There follows a long stretch of taxying to the refuelling point. Hercules 199 amiably ambles there and finally stops next to the waiting tankers. Waiting also is the RAF's man at Dulles.

Wing Commander David Farquhar, OC No.24 Squadron at the controls over Atlanta, Georgia.

But first US officials bustle aboard the plane. 'Got your crew list, Bud?' one addressed Don Ward. 'Here it is.' – 'Got two copies?' – 'Here's the second copy.' – 'Got your manifest?' – 'I just happen to have it with me.' Don keeps smiling.

As the customs men prod around his hold, the two pilots and navigator are driven to flight planning where they will prepare for the next stage of Monday's long journey. The flight engineer and loadmaster are already supervising the refuelling operation. No time is wasted.

David Farquhar takes over the captaincy from Andy Roberts for the second stage of the journey. Bill Moore continues as co-pilot. The pre-flight check begins and proceeds with noticeable briskness as befits having a Squadron Commander at the controls. The Dulles temperature in the high 80s may also have something to do with it. Someone mutters, 'Good training for where we are going.'

Astonishingly, Wing Commander Farquhar reverses the giant Hercules out of its parking space in a long curve. He then waits beside the runway for a Boeing to take-off before doing the same in a third of the distance. The State of Virginia is exchanged for Carolina during our steady climb.

At 20,000 feet there are new interesting cloud formations. Slim grey stratus clouds skim menacingly over white cumulus, like alien space ships on their way to invade a little all-American town. Suddenly these space ships vanish as swiftly as they appeared. Planet Earth is saved once more and Hercules 199 continued its imperturbable way southwards.

It passes over Georgia where a Federal army once marched from Atlanta to the sea. It glances down on townships and hamlets sweltering in the hot afternoon sunshine. Inside the aircraft, the temperature is pleasantly cool. Choosing his moment well, as usual, Don Ward produces chilled chicken sandwiches, acquired in Washington, followed by succulent seedless grapes. Everyone is appreciative and good-humoured. Those off-duty relax in their different ways.

'Navigators do crosswords,' I am told, 'while pilots read porn magazines.' It is not true, of course. The off-duty pilot on the top bunk is reading an aviation magazine.

All of a sudden the cloud conditions change for the worse. A ring of thunderheads, 20 miles in diameter, surround the aircraft. While Hercules 199 is now flying at 24,000 feet, they rise to over 45,000 feet. Many clouds have flattened peaks known as anvils, the tips of which extend for miles. 'Those are the kind of clouds,' David Farquhar informs me, 'that can pull an aircraft apart.'

View of cloud progressively building up across the Southern States of America.

Based on his long flying experience, he thinks ahead – calculating air speed and cloud drift. A slight change of course every so often and Hercules 199 slips between closing gaps. Below us Atlanta has been replaced by Jacksonville.

When the aircraft enters calmer Florida air space, oranges are produced and given to everyone.

'Beamed up,' it is suggested by an SF-minded serviceman.

Our route follows the western coast of Florida looking out across the Gulf of Mexico. We gaze down on rectangular fruit farms and irregular patches of glade water. A large US Air Force base appears ahead. Even its plan view, with runways pointing towards the Gulf, looks businesslike. A jet fighter shoots past us, streaks across the horizon, disappears.

Key West – the southernmost extent of the United States and resembling a fish hook of islands – is sighted. Over an island actually called Fish Hook, a new course is set to steer well clear of Cuba. The course takes the Hercules towards further cloud formations that seem to be bubbling up out of the sea. 'More plane crunchers,' David Farquhar remarks.

Key West, last island in the Florida chain and the southernmost point of the United States.

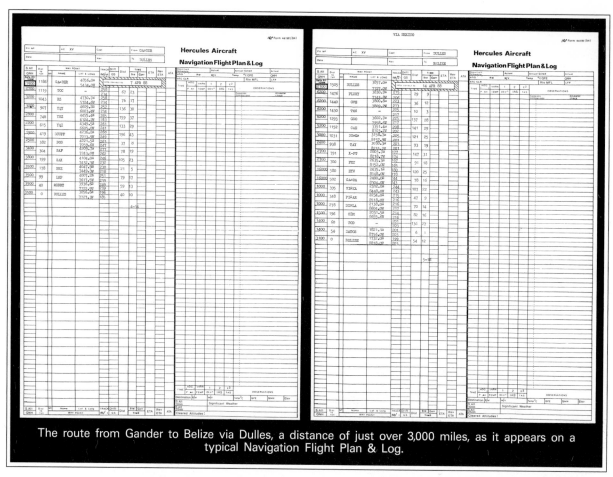

The route from Gander to Belize via Dulles, a distance of just over 3,000 miles, as it appears on a typical Navigation Flight Plan & Log.

The warming pan, which is the Gulf of Mexico and which sends the Gulf Stream all the way to Britain, also causes these clouds. They rise in knobbly pillars thousands of feet high. Again we edge our way round and between them.

Soon the coast of Mexico Yucatan is seen, a land of fire. Apart from the volcanoes, it is the time of year when the bush is burned. Flickering flames continue for mile after mile. The crew tell of smoke rising high into the upper air then hanging around for weeks. A faint acrid smell of burning fills the aircraft.

At the end of a long day's flying Hercules 199, piloted by Bill Moore, begins the let-down to its destination, Belize. With the Atlantic on the west and trouble-torn Central America lying on its other three sides, this small country – once British Honduras – still needs British support for its security. This is provided in many ways including protective Army units, Harrier jump jets and Puma helicopters, also Rapier missile sites to guard the airfield.

Belize airfield has a single runway. Because of the prevailing winds from the sea – the trade winds of sailing ship days – the approach to land is usually overland. Or rather over the thick rain forest.

From a mere 250 feet the forest, noted for some fearsome tropical creatures, looks too close for comfort. But to Bill Moore the landing is an application of his long training and flying experience to date. He puts the aircraft quietly down on the centre line of the runway. Reverse thrust follows, then a turn-off to the RAF parking area.

No sooner are the engines cut than the RAF presence in Belize makes itself felt. Royal

Air Force cars and vans, refuellers and mobile generators, converge on Hercules 199. The rear ramp is lowered and the off-loading of freight, brought all those miles from Wiltshire, begins.

Despite tropical heat and humidity, the work proceeds briskly, for not only has the large hold to be cleared, a full return load is waiting nearby to be put aboard – that night. At least the flying crew, after operating from dawn to dusk, is being relieved. Also for that night. 'There are taxis waiting to take you into town,' they are informed. 'Go, relax and enjoy yourselves.'

Relaxation means a meal at a restaurant overlooking the Spanish Main. Half the crew opt for sea food, the other half for steaks, plus a couple of beers apiece. All are well aware that they will be starting again at 0600 hours next morning.

Next morning, 0530 early-calls rouse crew members. They wash, shave and pack rapidly, then assemble in the hotel lobby where a welcome pot of coffee awaits them.

Role Equipper Andy Sample and Chief Technician Tucker Thompson commence morning checks before heat of the tropical day.

Cups are quickly filled and emptied because the taxis are outside.

Airmen and luggage pile into the taxis – old American cars that look like cartoons of old American cars. These automobiles rock and roll their way through the brief best part of town, the main, worst, part of town, over the Belize River and through ever-present forest to the airfield.

On arrival, crew members change into flying gear then tackle their separate yet inter-related duties. Pilots and navigator go to learn of the weather situation and to plan our flight back to Washington. Apparently the weather has become atrocious over the United States. Those clouds, seen rising yesterday from the Gulf of Mexico, are making their way up the Eastern Seaboard. Turbulence and thunderstorms await us. Plan A is to make for Washington. Plan B Philadelphia. Plan C anywhere we can land.

RAF personnel nod and get on with their work. Adrian Wilson systematically checks the Hercules airframe and engines. Don Ward closely inspects the freight brought aboard over-night. Again, the hold is tightly packed with little or no space left for returning servicemen.

Nearby a Puma helicopter is run up, cut and all is quiet again. Belize is not quite what it seems on the surface. Nearby also are Ayres Thrush aircraft, purpose-built crop spraying aircraft, usually used for the application of insecticides or fertilizers. In this case however, they are used to spray defoliants on drug-producing plants. 'The growers,' a Thrush pilot tells me, 'are the little men in the trade. They find a forest site and spend back-breaking

Above: Tapping the fuel tanks for water contamination. The tube lifts a valve and a fuel sample runs into the plastic bag.

Loadmaster Don Ward checking all nets, fastenings and tensioners on the overnight load.

Load detail 1. View looking aft on starboard side and showing tight fit along fuselage wall.

Load detail 2. View over top of freight which practically reaches the Hercules hold ceiling.

weeks clearing it. At last the area is ready for planting and the shoots appear. That is when we zap them.'

'What,' I ask glancing at a nearby pile of crashed planes, 'what about those?'

'They belonged to people,' he uses the past tense, 'who tried to fly into impossible clearings. Some of the wrecks are brought back here to discourage the others.'

I want to ask a lot more questions, but am being called for our own take-off. Today Flight Lieutenant Andy Roberts will be Captain and Wing Commander David Farquhar his Co-Pilot. Flying Officer Bill Moore will have a sort of day off – helping out at rest periods. Navigator Huw Thomas and Engineer Adrian Wilson are working as usual, as is Loadmaster Don Ward.

A small incident illustrates the understanding and quiet co-operation practised by the crew. While those concerned go through their pre-flight checks in the gathering heat of another tropical day, 'off-duty' Bill Moore makes some curious preparations. He adds a few drops of after-shave lotion to a tray of water, then dips lengths of paper towelling in the solution. These are wrung out and placed round the crew members necks to refresh them and absorb the sweat pouring down their faces.

After the pre-flight check and engine run-up, Hercules 199 is taxied to the inland end of the runway. There it turns and effortlessly takes off although heavily loaded.

The hot humid coast drops away as do the off-shore cays so beloved by yesterday's pirates and present day smugglers as well as holiday makers. Our climb takes us past low mist and high mist to a crystal-clear 27,000 feet.

Below: During long flight hours those off-duty tend to read paperbacks – 3 inches thick.

Half an hour after leaving Belize, Cuba can be seen along the southern horizon under a cap of clouds. Apart from these, the skies over the Gulf remain clear. Yesterday's storm clouds are now further north. They move slowly but inexorably and our Hercules will certainly catch up with them – a tortoise and hare race in reverse.

So the crew plans ahead for all contingencies. Details of alternative airports are produced and scrutinised. RAF flying procedures, contained in thick volumes, are studied. Despite the sun outside, the realities of men daring to fly remain ever present. Since Icarus fell, the best aviators emulate Daedalus.

The Florida Keys – as distinct from the Belize Cays – soon drift into view. From the air, the string of islands look much the same as on a well-coloured map. They are presented in verdant greens, the turquoise shades of shallow waters, the dark blues of the deeps. Intricately intermingled are houses, gardens and roads. One road continues on and on from island to island.

From Key West, Hercules 199 is banked on to a new heading, of almost due north. As yet the weather remains settled. Our journey proceeds above the eastern sunshine coast of Florida. The crew show me points of interest. To port are Orlando and Disneyworld. To starboard lie Cape Canaveral and Daytona Beach. But one has little time to stand and stare. An important end to the morning has arrived.

It is time for lunch. Don Ward produces an excellent chicken curry, its heat tempered by slices of tomato and cucumber. Cheese and biscuits follow, also Florida orange juice. What else when passing over that state?

After the meal come changeovers and rest periods. Andy Roberts stretches his legs in the hold as best he can around the freight and people there. Bill Moore, who is off-duty, reads an aviation magazine. Most of the passengers prefer thick best sellers to while away the long hours.

When Andy Roberts returns to his Captain's seat, David Farquar – still acting as Co-Pilot on this leg – occupies himself with some freshly picked mangoes. Somehow they have been put on the plane and arrive beside him at the right moment. Lovingly he selects, slices and savours them. Navigator Huw Thomas is never far from his desk, nor is Engineer Adrian Wilson easily distracted from his controls. Loadmaster Don Ward clears away the remains of lunches in one of those long plastic sacks that are more like galactic black holes. Every scrap of waste matter enters them and they are taken away at each port of call. Others help him. Hercules housekeeping is a continuous, collective, activity.

'Top of drop in five minutes,' Bill Moore informs us. This means our arrival at the far edge of the aerial plateau where 'cruise' becomes 'descent' beginning the let-down to Dulles. Once more the air waves become cluttered with cross-talk between aircraft and airports.

Every plane in the United States seems to be converging on or waiting above Washington DC. The reason for this is a great storm cloud lying over the airport and capital. All aircraft arriving at the former are stacked awaiting instructions. The city is being battered by torrential rain and has lost much of its electricity. Computers, indispensable to modern life, are out of action. 'Boy,' an air traffic controller speaks from his heart, 'have we got problems here!'

Just as our stacking looks like leading to diversion, a miracle takes place. The cloud mass shifts sideways leaving the airport clear. Aircraft encircling it are talked down with equally astonishing rapidity.

Soon it is the turn of our Hercules. We are banking and lining up with the duty runway when a light plane strays nonchalantly across our flight path. Muttered expletives are heard over the headsets. The little plane skitters off in another direction as if unaware it is near an international airfield and a particularly solid Hercules.

The return to Washington, after missing a rainstorm, for more freight, refuelling and ground checks.

Andy Roberts makes another perfect landing and taxies smoothly between civil airliners to the same parking space as on the previous day. The RAF man in Washington is first aboard with US officials close behind him. Don Ward again looks after the officials while transport and hotel arrangements are outlined to the crew.

There are, however, a couple of problems. The first involves filling the seemingly full hold further overnight. This will mean some personnel working late, also early next morning. The second problem is a technical one. An oil pressure unit on the propeller gearbox of No.3 engine has been giving trouble. Its replacement, requested from Lyneham, is due later by air freight, but will have to be fitted and tested.

Meanwhile transport to take the crew into Washington is waiting. The air-conditioned bus is much appreciated as the weather, despite the storm, remains hot and sticky.

The driver manoeuvres his bus through closely parked aircraft towards a high heavily-barred gate which could stop a battletank. Fortunately he has the correct piece of plastic to insert into a conveniently sited lock. Unfortunately, our run to Washington coincides with the late afternoon rush hour. It takes us well over an hour to reach the hotel.

What next? The evening is young as are the airmen released from their demanding duties. Washington is theirs for the night. What will they decide to do? It seems their minds are set on the same subject. At the hotel reception desk, one member asks the prettiest girl there a vital question, 'Is the Smithsonian Space Museum open this evening?' She is not sure and checks that it is on the telephone.

'Right,' everyone agrees. 'We'll meet back here in fifteen minutes.'

At the Smithsonian, the piece of Moon Rock is reverently touched on our way to the Samuel P. Longley Theatre. There they are showing the Space Shuttle film *The Dream is Alive*. For the next hour, mere airmen gaze enviously at astronauts on a screen that is five stories high. After that our party strolls to a bar for a couple of beers and some food. And so to bed.

Early next morning the crew assembles in the hotel lobby where Bill Moore – as part of his Co-Pilot duties – settles all bills. He does this with an officially held American Express card as he has done throughout the journey.

Despite heavy morning traffic in Washington, the bus arrives right on time. Conversation out to Dulles is about whether or not the oil pressure unit has arrived overnight. Horror stories are told of parts sent and what happened to them. I hear of the carefully packed and clearly labelled box that was empty. Of a unit which arrived safely, went into customs and was lost forever.

Immediately on our arrival at Dulles, the bus takes us to the RAF office. The box is there. Inside is another box. Inside that the required unit. 'Is it the right one?' asks an eternal cynic. 'Oh! ye of little faith,' someone replies. It is correct.

When the unit has been installed, Adrian Wilson runs No.3 engine and finds everything in order. The pilots and navigator are once again in Flight Planning.

Don Ward checks fasteners and tensioners on the crates brought aboard last night. Our Hercules will be near its maximum take-off weight of 160,000 lb. More horror stories are told of 170,000 lb take-offs from Ascension Island during the Falklands Campaign. Of Hercules after Hercules struggling out over the South Atlantic. 'If one engine had cut . . .'

The pilots and navigator come on board. Hercules 199 will be flying directly back to Lyneham. The trip of approximately 10 hours will mean arriving early in the morning. At, I am told, about 0400 hours.

After a full engine run-up, David Farquhar gives another impressive demonstration of how to taxi backwards. He then joins a queue of airliners waiting to take-off. Each jet plane busily shrieks along the runway before managing to get into the air. The turboprop Hercules lifts off far sooner as if empty.

The sky is heavily overcast, but Hercules 199 continues climbing like an enthusiastic mountaineer seeking the sun. At 5500 feet the welcoming sun is there. Its rays pour in through the many windows.

Today the clouds are more picturesque than menacing. David Farquhar leads us through the canyons while Don Ward decides we need lemon tea. The astringent scent of sliced lemon comes from the galley area. Cups move outwards, are sipped empty and pass back again to the disposal bag. I stand observing the Kingdom of the Clouds for hour after hour.

The clouds we had seen rising from the Gulf of Mexico warming pan on Monday; which had hit the Southern States and Washington yesterday on Tuesday; are heading for New York on Wednesday. We skirt the latest massif and continue towards Nova Scotia.

Travellers in this kingdom eat at odd times. Our 'breakfast' arrives early that afternoon in the form of grapefruit segments followed by warm croissants with Old English marmalade.

As we linger over our cups of coffee, afternoon wears toward evening. At 23,000 feet, the aircraft seems to be crawling above Novia Scotia. After passing Halifax, I watch both pilots simultaneously fold back the travelled parts of their maps and unfold further sections showing Newfoundland.

Don Ward sits by me doing his loadmaster's paperwork. He fills the multiplicity of spaces in the complicated forms with what seem like ancient hieroglyphics. Eventually he comes to the last form headed 'Main Meal'. Cartons covered in silver foil are transferred from a catering pack to the galley oven.

It is amazing how much is carried. Bags bulge with maps, shelves are stacked with manuals. There are headsets, oxygen masks, plugs and sockets everywhere.

I suddenly see an example of good housekeeping. A can of coke fizzes over part of the flight deck. Instantly the three people nearest to the spillage produce paper tissues and acting together carry out the mopping up operation.

The main meal of the day is served in the late evening. It consists of chilled melon, braised chicken with all the trimmings and fruit pie. Excellent at any time.

Which makes one think of time itself. During our journey the crew has coped with several times: Greenwich or Zulu, Universal, Standard, and Local. The last relates to the time within zones of longitude. If a complete country occupies a single zone, then it enjoys a common time. If, as many do, a country extends over several zones, then there may be time changes across that land as decreed by its government. The RAF uses Zulu Time and Army Local Time. 'Which explains', it is explained to me, 'why sometimes the two do not manage to meet.'

Time has other interesting aspects. We are flying over the North Atlantic on Midsummer's Day, so midnight is more like daylight. The spectacular sunset remains on the horizon. At the same time, a full moon rises seemingly out of the sea to float above the opposite horizon.

Don Ward observes engine run-up following the fitting of a new oil pressure transmitter unit.

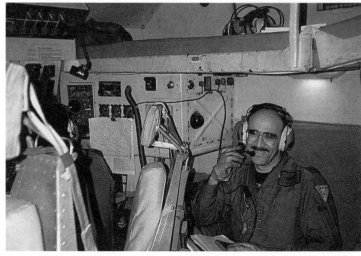

Above: Huw Thomas busy navigating Hercules 199 and undergoing his annual route check.

Above right: Squadron Leader Les Piper from the Hercules Training Squadron conducting Huw Thomas's route check.

Return to Lyneham Flight Planning. Captain Andy Roberts signs off with Bill Moore and Don Ward – at 0430 hours.

At last, day time is replaced by night time and man-made lights transform the flight deck – ceiling lights, wall lights, strip lights, spot lights and individual instrument lights. Dials glow. Radar screens appear to have acquired added fluorescence. Three dimensional crew members become flat black silhouettes. Their slight movements show they are unsleeping, maintaining contact with equally wide-awake air controllers.

The flight is nearly over. The lights of Shannon appear ahead welcoming us. From 27,000 feet, the Irish towns and villages make two-colour patterns. White lights glow in and around buildings, yellow street lights look like strands of golden tinsel..

What is left of the journey unreels rapidly. Eire and the sea are crossed in minutes, as is South Wales. 'Bristol,' Bill Moore nods towards a glittering star city.

'There's the Severn Bridge,' Adrian Wilson indicates a silver necklace over a silver river partly swathed in silver mist.

These magical scenes rise towards us as altimeter needles wind down aircraft heights from 6000 to 2000 feet. Sleeping Avon is followed by sleeping Wiltshire. Unsleeping Lyneham lies straight ahead. Captain David Farquhar talks quietly to Air Traffic Control who, in turn, have alerted Ground Handling. All the while, Hercules 199 is sliding down an invisible beam to the runway long before the airfield lights become visible.

Once again – as at Gander, Washington, Belize – a copybook landing is made. Tons of aircraft and freight return safely to earth. A short run and the Hercules is parked among its fleet companions.

The rest happens rapidly. Transport is waiting to take the crew to the Air Terminal building. There the Loadmaster goes to Customs, the Engineer visits Engineering, Pilots and Navigator look in at Flight Planning where it all began. Briefly they reassemble, mostly to exchange thanks and goodbyes for it is four in the morning. Debriefing will come later.

Outside, figures disperse across the car park. A voice from the darkness calls to me.

'Now you know a little of what we do at Lyneham.'

Index